"I'm Still Here"

"I'm Still Here"

✦

The Diary of a Driving Instructor

J. Myers

iUniverse, Inc.
New York Lincoln Shanghai

"I'm Still Here"
The Diary of a Driving Instructor

iUniverse, Inc.

For information address:
iUniverse, Inc.
2021 Pine Lake Road, Suite 100
Lincoln, NE 68512
www.iuniverse.com

ISBN: 0-595-28029-3

Printed in the United States of America

Individual deductions will vary. Common Sense and going by the legal rules of the road while better understanding your surroundings is the key point of Safety. Jump Starting a car is Dangerous. It can cause physical damage. It can also cause electrical damage. "The Key Must Be Removed and The Owners Manual Checked Prior To Any Repair Procedure." Always Remember…If you drink, you should not drive.

Static Electricity can cause a fire at the gas pump. If you keep getting in and out of the car, you could build up a static charge. Touch the metal when your feet are on the ground, this should discharge the static build up. Ask your parents, teachers or friends what they think about this. Remember…Never be afraid to ask a question. It's not the question, It's the answer that you might not be ready for.

Special Update.…Every year new ideas and improvements are made to new model cars and trucks. One idea or improvement may be in the way you are required to check the fluids in your car. It could be a different suggested way to check the power steering fluid or the transmission fluid or even the battery. YOU MUST CHECK THE OWNERS MANUAL BEFORE YOU EVEN OPEN THE HOOD. DO NOT, FOR ANY REASON, FEEL BAD ABOUT ASKING QUESTIONS. YOU MAY HAVE THE ONE CAR THAT REQUIRES A DIFFERENT TYPE OF ATTENTION. DON'T TAKE THE CHANCE OF CHECKING SOMETHING THE WRONG WAY. PLEASE, READ YOUR OWNERS MANUAL FIRST.

Thanks a lot Theresa.

Patience contributed by my wife, Diane.

                    Thank You.

            A special note to my Uncle Lud.

Special Note: You must let your car warm up before you drive it. You will learn a lot of things to do and learn a lot about the things around you as you learn to drive. The information in this publication is only a drop in the bucket. If you listen to everyone's ideas, then add your own insight, you will find that safety is the number one priority when it comes to driving. You cannot operate a motor vehicle if you are under the legal driving age in your state. There is no way around it. It is against the law.

Contents

This is the introduction page and I don't know how to start. I thought that actual student comments should be added and so they have.

I would like to say something to you before you turn the page, and that is,

Always Remember…people can call you any name they want, But they can call you at home in the morning. Thinking about your personal safety is not selfish. Thinking about your personal safety is what we call Common Sense.

A note of interest is the 3 and 9 hand to wheel position to be used while operating an air bag equipped vehicle. Just because you have an air bag does not mean you shouldn't know how to turn the wheel hand over hand and recover. When you drive, you must get all the information you can and then make your own decision.

Everyone has an opinion. You can listen to it, but it's up to you to find the real truth. Seatbelts do save lives. Soon the law will require everyone in the car to wear a seatbelt at all times.

P.S.

Never attempt to do repairs on a car without checking The Owners Manual First. Don't touch any car without direct permission from The Coherent Vehicle Owner.

NEVER DRINK AND DRIVE AND ALWAYS READ THE LABELS ON ALL MEDICATIONS FOR SIDE EFFECTS THAT MAY AFFECT YOUR ABILITY TO DRIVE.

Notice

As said in your driver's manual, you must have a legal permit and a legal senior licensed operator with you when you drive a car, as specified by law.

The driver's manual explains the laws and you agree to go along with them.

For best results, ask questions. Don't be afraid to ask.

The explanations in this book are meant for food for thought only. We've all seen keys turned. If you turn a key, you better be legal. If anything happens, and you are not legal, it is all your fault. Legal = OK. Not legal = Your fault. It's just that easy.

Just take your time and use common sense.

Remember…Always Think Safety.

—**The Author**

Chapter 1

STUDENT COMMENTS

In Drivers Ed., I have learned to use hand over hand while turning. I used to let the wheel slide through my hands, but I see that hand over hand is much safer and gives me more control. Also, my gas mileage has increased. I allow my car to coast when I see that there is a stopped car or a red light in front of me. I now let the car settle down, then move to the brake instead of braking at the last minute. I also learned to check my blind spot. Before, I would only use the inside mirror when merging. Also, when stopping, I now look to the inside mirror to make sure the car behind me is also stopping.

***

During Drivers Ed., I have learned to use my rear view mirror more often, check my blind spot and be more aware of my surroundings in a driving situation. I have become more cautious and aware of other cars and learned techniques of defensive driving that will help me on the road. I have also enjoyed our food stops and singing for you in the back of the car. "Carvel Rules," "Thank you for helping me become an Improved Driver."

***

What did I learn in Drivers Education? To answer this question, I have to look back on to the beginning of the semester. When I started Drivers Ed., I was insecure and I did not have much confidence behind the wheel. The skills learned in this course that stand out are the use of the inside mirror, the speed control, ability to drive under any conditions. My parents also have benefited because my mileage per tank has increased. Thank you.

***

I feel more comfortable on highways and when changing lanes. I also learned when to let the car settle down and how to drive on hills and other tricky areas.

***

I learned in Drivers Ed. that a lot more things go on around you than you think and you must be aware of everything. I've also learned that the people in the car with you could be a distraction. For instance when you kept moving my mirror, Mr. Myers. I learned that all drivers must be considerate of the others. That most of the time it's not the other person that's at fault.

Thank You Mr. Myers for your patience with the Saturday Class that I switched out of.

Have a nice summer.

***

STUDENT COMMENTS

I think the one thing that the Driving part of Drivers Ed. helped me to do was check blind spots, drive under stress, and find out how to get home in unfamiliar territory. I also got useful information on highway travel. I was taught how to feel comfortable on the highway, which I couldn't before Drivers Ed.

***

There are many things that I learned in the Driving part of Drivers Education. I learned that "Signals are mechanical and subject to failure." I learned to always watch out for the other cars making stupid mistakes. I should always be aware of everything on the road and off the road. I should drive defensively at all times and not assume that everybody else on the road has taken Drivers Ed. and knows what they are doing.

***

I believe the most important lesson learned in this segment of Drivers Ed. was that of observation, the importance of constantly looking in all directions possible while maintaining one's concentration on the road. Either by looking at the blind spot when changing lanes or in the inside mirror before entering a potentially hazardous situation, or just looking around when stopped. Situational awareness is the most vital part of driving safely.

***

I became more relaxed with driving in general. I saw a great deal more as Drivers Ed. went on. I'm more comfortable with busy areas, braking and highway driving. I notice stop signs, kids and potential hazards. I fear no road.

***

I feel that I have learned a lot about my own driving and driving in general. My wheel control has improved and I also greatly improved my "Scanning ability." I have a better overall view of "The Total Picture" now. I also have a better understanding of other driver's errors.

***

Dear Mr. Myers,
    Drivers ED. was surprisingly good. I have increased my general confidence in all areas of driving. I especially have no problems with getting on highways. I feel positive with my driving and satisfied with the course.

***

What I always heard and finally learned was to check the inside mirror as an automatic reflex.

***

STUDENT COMMENTS

What I remember most, To look in the mirror when I stop, wheel control and not to get too close to the car in front of me.

***

Through Drivers Education I learned to use the inside mirror efficiently and to check over my shoulder for blind spots. This increased my awareness of cars, things, and people around me. I also learned to listen to my surrounding environment while driving.

***

As a result of Drivers Education, I have learned to be a cautious driver and help to preserve peace on the road. I have learned how to change lanes on a highway because I'm now aware of my blind spot and being aware to other drivers on the road. The ultimate challenge for me was to pass my road test and Drivers Education thoroughly prepared me for it and I passed. I think this demonstrates the tremendous growth I under went as a new driver.

***

Since Drivers Education I feel much more comfortable driving. Something that stands out very strongly, that I always think of while driving, is looking into my rear view mirror before I come to a stop. Whether at a stop sign, or a stop light, or just slowing down, I always look in my mirror first. I also drive much closer to the speed limit, and have Much better wheel control. I'm always using hand over hand.

***

I learned more than I thought I would during the driving portion of Drivers Education. I learned how to conserve gas and to be a safer driver. I learned how to drive on the highway, merge, and change lanes correctly. My skills have improved and my awareness of what is going on around me has increased. I've developed a sense of direction. I really know how to get around now and I appreciate all the time and effort that Mr. Myers took in teaching me.

Thanks.

***

My gas mileage has increased
I'm more focused
I drive slower
I (usually) come to a full stop
I look around instead of straight ahead
I can find my way home on the highway when I get lost.

***

Welcome to the driving portion of Driver's Ed. It's never advised to use hand gestures to another driver. Your vocabulary can turn a small situation into a virtual firefight. People get all frantic, know what I mean. You must be able to vent your frustrations. It's not easy to hold your emotions back at times. In other situations it might be alright to voice an open opinion, within limits. You must be the judge of that.

***

You are now entering a training vehicle, riding with new students. "I am not hard to get along with," is my way of putting across to the students that the fact of the matter is, I don't care what you think you know you are here to learn. I will annoy you into learning. I will trick you into learning. This is a no holds barred situation. So, get ready to learn.

The inside mirror is my pet. I can detect motion in the mirror out of the corner of my right eye as I drive. Some students pick up the use of the inside mirror faster than others do. I have found that if reference points are used correctly, the student will react to them by keeping their concentration closer to themselves. Being able to judge distance is very important. You must use your depth perception all of the time.

It seems that tunnel vision is evident in all of the students today. They all seem to use their directional, which is good. They all speed and I think it is because of tunnel vision. They are all racing to nowhere. No one knows how to stop before stop lines. Scanning the intersection is not done correctly if done at all. A lot of basic safety rules are not followed. One of the rules is to always proceed with caution. It is funny in a way because they think that they can drive. Wheel control is a direct copy of someone else and far from acceptable. The problem is that they were never taught the right way in the beginning. You do not just turn the wheel, you work the wheel.

You guide the car; the car does not guide you. One student found it hard to stay in the lane correctly with his hands on the bottom of the wheel. I told him to put his hands up on the wheel and the problem was solved.

You must have good wheel control. The 10 o'clock position with the left hand, and the 2 o'clock position with the right hand. This is how you drive a car. You cannot control the car with your hands down on the wheel. This student also has a very bad habit of going directly from the gas to the brake. You must develop a pause between the two pedals as much as possible.

Stopping distance is good. They are all open-eyed and show interest, I think that I might have a good group here.

***

Here we are again. Today is Tuesday and the students all seem to have a different set of things wrong with their driving. The being nervous part seems to be the biggest problem with this group. This leads to tunnel vision.

Tunnel vision is also triggered by poor wheel control, and they all have poor wheel control. These students differ in their reaction times, but they all show interest, so that's a good start. Attitudes are good, and without a good attitude, you should not be behind the wheel.

The speed factor is at least 10 MPH over the posted limit. This creates very bad tunnel vision. These new drivers have not memorized enough items to be comfortable yet. They stop at intersections where they can see. You are required by law to stop before the stop-line first. Then you can roll up and stop again where you can see that it is clear to go.

The stop-line is a big thing. You must respect the rules of the road to stay safe. The stop-line is the wide white or maybe a yellow line that starts at the curb and goes out to about the center of the road.

***

This is the subject called driving, so lets start thinking. Take your house for example. Out of which window do you have the very best view of the road? Intersections with traffic lights are the best to go by. Maybe you can see a stop sign situation better from an upstairs window. You have to check it out. If no intersections or stop signs can be seen, a turn in the road can be used to judge the flow of traffic. The speed of the flow of traffic is affected by many different factors that can pop up at any time in any combination. You can tell a lot by the sounds of the flow of traffic.

Listen for the sound the car is making. You have a combination of sounds, not just one. The motor makes a sound and the tires also contribute but with a different sound. The exhaust system adds yet another tone. Windshield wipers make more noise as they go faster, then add the sound of the water being displaced. The water on the road makes the sound of the tires different. Slush and snow also have a way of adding on muffling sounds. Air displacement creates its own sound. These different sounds should be memorized. The more you memorize, the safer you are. "But It Will Take Time."

If you look at a fixed object about seven feet off the ground when you first hear a car. Then, when you see the car out of the corner of your eye, take one fast glance at the car and then back to the fixed object at the seven-foot point. As the car passes, you can judge its approximate speed by the time it takes the length of the car to pass the fixed object. This takes practice and patience.

Remember…Sounds are the foundations of many conditioned reflexes. Looking out a window is one thing, driving is another.

After a few months driving time, you will start to be able to judge the flow of traffic much easier.

Remember…Even odds the drivers around you have more driving time and will take advantage of your insecurity. Stay to the right as much as possible. "Do not challenge right of way." Consider yourself low man on the totem pole. Knowledge and actual application of knowledge differ enormously, so you have to take your time.

Don't try to push or you might get shoved. When it comes to driving, "personalities change."

Always Remember…You can think what you want, but be careful of what you say.

The maintenance of the vehicle is the responsibility of the owner. But, if you borrow a car and you get a ticket because of a bad tire, the ticket is your responsibility. If you get stopped for speeding, you get the ticket. The problem does not stop there. The insurance company can see the action as a threat and raise your insurance rate. If you borrow something, it usually means that you do not have it with you or you do not own one of your own. When you borrow a car, you treat it with Kid Gloves. If you get a lot of tickets with your parents' car, it will cause them heartache and financial aggravation.

Remember…What goes around comes around.

So go bring in the dog and put out the cat. Then get comfortable where you are sitting and understand that information does not need to be a bore.

Remember…Safety First and Never Drop Your Guard!

***

You must know the dimensions of the vehicle you are driving. You are actually becoming a small machine operator and with this you take full responsibility for your actions.

Getting into the habit of asking your passengers to check the tires as they enter the car not only helps the driver out, but it also plants a seed of thought in the passengers mind that could grow into a "conditioned reflex." The person may start to get into the habit of checking the tires automatically. It is not that we forget, it is just that we do not think to check. This is called taking something for granted. Because you assume everything is Ok and Ok is not a problem or a threat to you, you just go about your business giving it no further thought. It is what we refer to as "out of sight, out of mind."

The spare tire is a different story. You do not see this tire unless you open the trunk, and even then it might be covered up or hidden away. Valve extensions are used to extend the existing valve stem, making it easier to put air into the tire. A spare tire should never be stored with a valve extension on it. The problem is that the extension could press against the trunk mat causing the tire to deflate slowly.

Air pressure can be easily misjudged. Tire gauges are inexpensive. You can buy one at any auto parts store. Keep it in the car. You can't rely on incorrect tire pressure readings. "Buy brand name tools with a guarantee!" You have to start to outfit your own toolbox. Do not carry a lot of junk.

Low profile tires do not have far to go to be flat, so extra attention must be given if you have these tires on your car. You have to be sure that the tires you want to see on your car will fit correctly. The wrong size wheel could rub against the fender or cause steering problems.

Backing into the curb will cause damage to your tires and rims. With low profile tires, the chances of wheel damage become much greater. Know your car and take good care of it. If you do, you will enjoy years of peace of mind when you travel.

Remember…You are getting your license now, but you are going to be driving for a long time, so take your time.

***

You will hear people say that they really do not like to read. If you do not like to read, it is usually because you do not like what you are reading. I hope you find this accumulation of ideas easy to read.

Paying attention to the cars around you is a must. If you see a car with the back end raised up higher than the front, try to stay away from it. Raising the back of the car will increase the chance of a gas tank rupture in an accident situation. Most cars today are front wheel drive but a lot of older rear wheel drive cars are still around.

Raising the back of the car creates problems for the driver while rounding turns. When you change the center of gravity, the rear end has a much greater chance of breaking traction, causing the car to slide off the road.

Maybe, if your lucky, the car will skid around in a complete circle and you can regain control, maybe not. If you are planning to lift the rear of the car to accommodate over-sized tires, I recommend changing the rear wheel wells and buying special rims. You may have to change the gas tank. It all depends on how much you want to get into it.

With this method, the back of the car is sure to give better traction and stability. At the same time, it will not affect the center of gravity that much.

Another problem with raising the rear and its effect on braking, is when you try to stop, the rear end lifts up even more, placing more weight on the front end. Now the front brakes will have to do a lot more work to slow the car down.

Most cars have disk brakes on the front and drum brakes on the rear. Disk brakes will lock up first if emergency pressure is applied. The rear wheels can continue to turn two maybe three more rotations before enough surface to surface pressure stops the wheel. The A.B.S. system or anti-lock system is designed to pulsate the braking pressure. The disc system has been used in the aircraft business for years and has well proven its effectiveness. The shoe and drum system has been around a long time.

Remember…4 wheel disc brakes are the best.

Please keep in mind that anything mechanical is subject to failure. You must be mentally prepared for any system's failure. Be calm and stay relaxed. No matter how many years you have been driving, brake failure will freak you out.

***

When you have new tires put on your car, question any over use of the impact wrench. The mechanic might be using this compressed air driven tool to tighten the lug nuts on your wheels when they are put back onto the car.

"The problem is the air pressure." If the pounds of pressure are too high, the lug nuts will be over-tightened. The metal rim is cold when it is put on the car. As you drive, the metal heats up and expands. This can cause problems when it comes to changing a flat tire. You could find yourself somewhere with a flat tire and not be able to remove the lug nuts with the lug wrench supplied to you by the manufacturer of the car.

New tires must be balanced. The tire is put on a balancing machine. This machine shows where small lead weights are to be fastened to the rim to insure smoother tire rotations. A tire that is out of balance will cause premature tire wear. An out of balance tire can be felt as a small vibration in the steering wheel. It seems to go away as the speed is increased. Mind you now, this or any other abnormal vibration that is felt during the operation of any piece of machinery must be attended to immediately. If you hear a small noise, it is going to turn into a bigger noise. Check it out when you first hear it.

Remember…You are not satisfied until you know exactly what the sound is. It might not be anything to worry about or it could be the start of a bigger problem. It will cost you less for repairs if you catch the problem early.

Valve stems should be checked carefully. The valve stem is the apparatus used to hold the air in the tire. If the valve stem has a cut or a slice, it should be changed. What you are looking at is a situation where the air could be leaking out so slowly that you just do not notice it until it is dangerously low or all the way flat.

Remember…The radial tire can sometimes give the impression of being under-inflated when actually the tire pressure is correct. If you keep putting air into it until the tire looks good to the eye, you will cause premature tire wear. Get your tire gauge out and check it yourself.

If you have new valve stems installed when you buy new tires, make sure they do not stick out like a sore thumb. If you question the use of what seems to be very long valve stems, and are told they are better or they were all that were on hand at the time, do not feel shy about telling the service manager that you will bring the car back the next day to have the correct length valve stems installed At No Extra Cost, Thank You!

Just like anything else, if you are not happy with the answer that you get, "Ask to talk to someone higher up!"

If you go back to where you bought the tires the next day, make sure you are not charged again for the new valves. "Valve stems can be removed and used again."

To check to see if you have a slow leak in the valve or maybe a loose valve, take the valve cap off and spit some saliva onto the end of your finger. Then spread it over the now exposed valve. If there is a leak, it will show as air bubbles.

If you are testing for a leak with the tire off of the car and lying flat on the ground, water can be used. With the tire on the car, saliva works in a pinch. Valve caps must have no cracks and must fit well. Plastic caps are the best ones. Metal valve caps can be easily over-tightened and pliers may be needed to remove them. Stay away from metal caps.

***

Because this is general information, lets talk about gas gauge problems. You are driving along and notice you are low on gas. Some gauges have lights that go on to indicate to the driver that it is time to get gas. I like the indicator light myself because it is noticed by the passenger and brought to the attention of the driver. Your passengers are your co-pilots. Your place is in the captain's chair.

If you are a passenger and notice the low fuel indicator is indicating, tell the driver. A good co-pilot relays information. This information is better placed in the form of a question. You do not want to step on the driver's toes, so to speak. You must remember that every driver's ego is affected differently by different driving situations. Asking the driver what the light means is the best way of relaying the information. Then to keep the channel of communication open, you could say that you like the idea of a low fuel indicator. This will turn the driver's concentration back to driving the car. A passenger means teamwork, not a distraction. If you cannot help, do not help. If you notice the light goes on, you must pick the right time to bring it to the attention of the driver.

When a car goes around a turn, the gasoline goes from side to side in the tank. This may cause the light to come on for a moment. This is not the time to yell out, "Gas Gauge!" You could distract the driver and cause an accident. Take your time, you will figure it out. Remember… Be Polite!

This thing called driving is not just turning the key and go. You must have a lot of common sense to drive a car safely. It is not a joke. Use the correct grade of gasoline for your car. If you pull into a gas station and see a big tanker truck delivering fuel to the station, pull out of the station and find another one. However, in an emergency, buy any gasoline that is available to you. Do not fill up your tank if you do not have to.

Gasoline is stored in large tanks underground. When fuel is added to the underground tanks, it stirs up the sediment at the bottom of the tank. "You should wait a few hours before buying gasoline from that station."

I have seen situations where cars have taken on fuel and then two blocks or so later, the motor just stopped running.

This becomes a nightmare for the driver. They know that they have fuel, but do not realize that the new fuel is the problem. If this ever happens, go back to where you got the gas and explain the situation to the station manager. The gas station is responsible for this occurrence. This problem should be corrected by the gas station at no cost to you. Remember…You did not buy a tank of water, you paid good money for a tank of gasoline. "Get what you pay for."

Full-service means that the attendant is to check all the fluid levels. Brake fluid, transmission fluid, engine oil level, power steering fluid and windshield washer fluid. The coolant level and the battery are to be checked also. Tire pressure is also checked and the windows are to be cleaned. If you have any problem with this service, ask to speak to the manager. This may not be a full-service gas station.

Self-service is just what it sounds like. You exit the vehicle and pump the gas yourself. The instructions are on the pump. If you have a problem, ask an attendant for assistance. With full-service, wait until the attendant has finished pumping the gas before handing over your cash. If you pay first, you stand a chance of pulling away from the pump in the middle of fueling. These things do happen to people.

You may have to walk up to the window and place the money in the sliding, metal draw and tell the attendant the amount of fuel you want. For example, it would sound like this, "Five-dollars, 87 octane on pump number 4, please." It is nice to be polite. The pump will automatically stop when it comes up to five dollars. Don't forget to press the 87 button on the pump. Most cars run well on 87 octane, but be on the safe side and check your owner's manual.

If the gas pump is manually operated, this means that you have to stop the pump by releasing the handle when the pump reads almost the amount. Then by squeezing the handle a little at a time, bring the numbers up to the correct amount. Shut the pump off. Remove hose from the car and secure it to the gas pump. Most pumps today are automatic. You just have to hold the handle until it stops by itself.

With full-service, the attendant will ask you how much you want and he/she will put it in the tank. You do not give the attendant the money until after the gas has been pumped. I know of a situation where a young lady gave the attendant the money first and after pumping the gas, the attendant claimed that she had not already paid. The attendant threatened to call the police if the driver did not pay. Be careful; buy your gas in the daytime. By the way, the young lady had to pay twice for the gas. She was not a happy camper to say the least.

***

You should know your car. Engine oil is to be added by the quart. Transmission fluid is measured by the pint. To check the motor oil, the motor must be shut off. To check the transmission fluid level, the motor must be running. If the attendant checks your transmission and heads to your car with a quart of transmission fluid, you had better get out of the car and see what is going on. Transmission fluid is added by pint measurement, not by quart. ALWAYS READ YOUR OWNERS MANUAL FIRST.

If you over-fill the transmission, it will destroy the software and cost you a new or rebuilt transmission. This can be a hard thing to prove, so it is up to you to double-check. After you close the hood, you stop thinking about it and all of a sudden it is too late. When transmission fluid is added from a quart container, it must be added a little bit at a time and checked after each little bit is added.

Remember…Over-filling will cause transmission failure.

Now, if you are checking things yourself, you will notice that there is an over flow tank on the side of the radiator. This has a cold and a hot mark on it. It **should not** be filled to the top just because it may look low.

Do not remove the radiator cap when the motor is running. Antifreeze is added to the over flow tank and not into the radiator. This reduces the chance of the hot antifreeze spraying up onto your face, neck, arms, chest and stomach. Read your owner's manual. The radiator cap has a safety catch to it. It is only to be removed when the motor is cold. That does not mean after a quick trip to the store.

When you check the oil level, the motor must be shut off. If the motor is running, the oil is being sloshed back and forth in the oil pan causing inaccurate oil level readings.

REMEMBER…THE CAR MUST BE IN PARK AND THE PARKING BREAK MUST BE ON WHEN YOU ARE UNDER THE HOOD OF YOUR CAR!

With rag in hand, locate the dipstick. The dipstick is long; it goes down into the oil pan. As you remove the stick, wipe it clean with a rag. Do not let the oil on the stick drip off onto the motor. Droplets of oil on the exhaust manifold will cause some smoke, but no fire. On the end of the dipstick you have two lines. The lower line is low and the upper line is full. Make sure you wipe the stick clean or you will not get an accurate oil level reading.

If any oil drips on the car, clean it off right away. "Do not over-fill" is stamped right on the dipstick and it means what it says. Let's just say you have a slight oil leak and have made plans to have it fixed when suddenly you are required to make a longer than average road trip, do not make a mistake with this. Never over-fill the oil before the trip thinking this will balance out the oil you are going to lose.

If you have this problem, plan to stop at the halfway point or sooner and re-check the oil level. Mind you now, if you see oil constantly dripping, by this I mean a steady drip, drip, drip, the car should not be driven any further than for repairs. Maybe a tow truck might be better advised. It's your decision.

After wiping the stick clean, put it back into the motor and pause for a moment before removing the stick again. This time when you pull the stick out, pull it out nice and easy so the reading will be correct. Make sure you keep the end of the stick pointed down. If you hold the end of the dip stick up in the air to read it, the oil on the end will run down the stick giving you a false oil level reading. When you take it out, you must hold it away from you and down.

Sometimes we do not catch things right away. If it seems that the stick is fighting back, Do Not Force It! Instead, remove the stick and wipe it clean again. You may be trying to move too fast. Watch how it comes out so you will not have this problem. If it will not go back in at all, Do Not Force It! There may be someone around to give you a hand. You cannot leave the dipstick out. Some sticks have a finger loop to make them easier to remove.

Others have a tee handle. Some even have the word "oil" written on them. If what you remove resembles a cap with "oil" written on it, put it back on. This is where you add oil, so put it back on and make sure it is on tight.

If you are buying a car, ask the dealer or seller to demonstrate how to check the oil. With family matters, ask parents to lend a hand. If you do not know, ask! If you do not ask, you may never know.

You must make sure the stick is in all the way. Sticks have seals or small cap-type covers at the top and if the stick is not in all the way, you will not get an accurate oil level reading.

Old oil is a dark color and can be seen on the stick easily. New oil is more along the lines of clear and may be harder to see. By turning the stick and checking the back, you can find the level by thinking wet or dry. The metal on the backside of the stick is less polished and darker in color, making it easier to determine where the dry ends and the thin coat of oil begins. Then just compare one side to the other.

The space between the lines on the stick in fluid measurements is one quart. Add oil to your car a quart at a time, only when needed. If you are going on a long trip, make sure that you have extra oil with you. If you develop a problem down the road, you can add oil and at least get off the highway to a safer location. Buying oil on the road is expensive.

You have to keep track of the gauges and warning lights on the dashboard when you drive. Detecting a warning light can deter engine failure. If you do not pay attention, the repair bill could be more than you can handle or more than the car is worth. Whereas; if you pay attention to your means of transportation you will experience years of motoring fun, unless someone steals your car. This has been known to happen.

Remember…Add oil by the quart. If you add oil in little drips and drabs, the chances of over-filling are excellent. Wait until the oil level is at the low mark to add oil. Add it one quart at a time. Do not let the oil level stay low for any reason. The next time you add a quart of oil, write down the mileage and see how far you go until you have to add another quart.

The oil cap is removed to add oil, then must be replaced. This is another item that must be kept track of. There is a lot to do, huh? It usually twists off and is located somewhere on the upper portion of the motor. Most of the time it is on the valve cover. The operator's manual should show a picture and give an explanation. It should say, "If you over-fill, you must take some out!"

You must tell your parents right away. This is not a situation where, "When I drive the extra oil will be used up anyway." Or "If I do not look at it, it will go away." It is not going anywhere. Anyone can make a mistake. Mistakes are the main part of our learning system. We learn by our mistakes, if we admit to making them.

You may be thinking that if you tell your parents they will yell at you and not let you use the car again. Well, if you do not tell them, there might not be a car to borrow. Do not do that to yourself.

If your parents go ballistic, give them time to come back down to earth. Then you might want to start to stand a bit taller. You have developed a major conditioned reflex. You are over the fear of telling the truth.

With machinery, if a problem situation enters the picture, it is to be corrected as soon as it is detected. I would like to repeat that. It is to be corrected as soon as it is detected.

***

If you pay with a credit card, make sure that you get the card back before you sign the charge form. Remember to get the carbon paper if there is one, and destroy it. If the carbon paper falls into the wrong hands, another card could be made and the charges made could be your responsibility.

Read the small print. Make sure that if this were to happen, the false charges would not be held against you. If you lose a credit card, you must call the credit card company right away. Some cards have and extra insurance policy to cover loss and theft. You have to check it out.

Prices at the gas pumps are higher for credit card purchases than they are for cash purchases. If you pay with cash and use self-service pumps, you will get the best deal. It is nice to have a credit card for emergency situations only.

Now you have gas to go and brakes to stop, but where do you stop?

* "The Stop Line." You must stop before this line. Then after a full stop, which consists of a 2 to 3 second pause, you are allowed to roll forward until you can see and then stop again. When you stop, you must stop with the front end of your car before the stop line. That is how it is done. As you start to drive, you will learn real quick that cars will make turns over the end of the line, into your lane. If you stop over the stop line, you could get a ticket. If you are still on probation, it could mean a suspension of your driving privileges.

On the front of the car you have a bumper. It sticks out the farthest. The steering wheel controls the direction of the front wheels. Because we relate more to the steering than the dimension of the car, we have a tendency to stop with our front wheels where our front bumper should be. This is an easy habit to get into and a hard one to break. The front bumper is to be before the stop line when you stop.

I have also noticed that there is a tendency to bring the foot to the brake before checking the inside mirror. I cannot understand why the inside mirror cannot be checked faster than you can get your foot from the gas to the brake. Your eyes are your main source of information.

***

Moving to another day we find a student with a speed and distance problem. He sees a green light down the road and continues to stay on the gas. If you see a green light in the distance, by the time you get close to it, it will probably change to yellow and then to red. You must expect it to change. This is called a stale green light.

Next we have a young lady who refers to herself as a brunette blond. This might be an attitude problem, we will just have to wait and see. Another student in the same group shows excellent potential. You have to remember that peer pressure is a big problem with new drivers. Until they find their own pace, they will try to outdo everyone else in the car, including the instructor.

I move the students inside mirror once in awhile to get them to correct it while driving without going off the road or hitting something around them. One student moved my mirror after I moved hers. Instead of resetting her mirror she chose to be cute and move mine. It turns out that she was a friend of a former student of mine that moved my mirror once as well. This former student was very shy in the car and after many weeks of mirror correcting, she got up the nerve to move mine. Everyone in the car laughed and from that day on, her attitude changed. The ice had been broken. She opened up and we had excellent communication between everyone in the car. Just like flipping a switch, she decided to become a person, it was nice to see. It is an open acceptance of the situation, or maybe it just took me to break the ice.

This new student was trying to make some kind of cute impression when in fact she made a very bad impression. Cute to me is an attitude and there is no place for cute attitudes when you drive.

Another student started the car then put the left directional on before taking it out of park. You change gears from park to drive with your foot pressing the break. Then you must put the directional on. Standard operating procedures must be memorized to insure maximum safety. We seem to be developing a pattern here.

To break it down, it consists of observation, judgement and control. It takes a little bit of time for the students to get used to each other. It also takes a little bit of time to get used to the car. So far it looks like a good group.

***

Today the trend seems to be the same. Poor wheel control, nervous students, stop line problems and stop sign problems. Rolling after a stop is also a problem with this group. The way to correct this problem is simple. When you come to a full stop, you must not let the car roll. Because you ease off the brake to make for a smoother stop, it becomes easy to forget that after you make a smooth stop, you must re-apply pressure to the brake to keep the car stationary.

Most of the students in this class do not understand how to use the inside mirror at all. Lane changing needs work and this is basically because of the blind spot. The ones that check their blind spots have a problem staying in the center of the lane. They take the directional off too soon, if it is used at all.

I have noticed false starts now and then. A false start is good in stock car racing, but it's a bluff. It makes the other cars think that you are stopping, then when they slow down, you go. This gives you a jump on the pack. Out on the road, you could get hurt real quick pulling a false start. You must be positive that the car in front of you is really pulling away from you before you consider going anywhere. Do not rush, you are still trying to learn. It takes time to master the common sense part of driving.

Stopping distance overall with this group is good. You must see road between the front end of your car and the rear bumper of the car stopped in front of you. You cannot count the road under the car in front of you unless you plan to use it. If you plan to use the space under the car in front of you, you better be driving a very flat car.

So, on to another class. I am going to have a lot of work to do with the inside mirror with this class. One student tried to come to a stop as he was resetting the inside mirror. Later, I moved the inside mirror again and he put on a real show trying to stay in his lane and set the mirror at the same time. I did notice as he worked for control his speed dropped. That tells me that I have broken his tunnel vision. Now, I have the peripheral vision to set into place. This student has a good attitude. That will be very helpful. With the next student, well, you name it and it is there. Poor wheel control, bad observation and judgement. She makes turns over the end of the yellow line. She makes turns over the end of stop lines. I asked her to check her mirror and she checked the outside mirror.

I have a lot of people here that do not know what they are doing. Most of these students have licenses and think that they are doing just great. They all speed and do not use their directional at all. You name it and this class has it. No one checks the inside mirror when they stop and most of them just do not seem to care. This is another indication of tunnel vision.

We need to take into consideration the fact that each generation has a responsibility to the next. Each year more cars find their way onto the roads and the speed and concentration of the flow of traffic is increasing.

Note. If power steering fluid is added and a new container is opened, they probably will charge you the cost of the full container. Make sure that when the attendant is finished adding the fluid to your car, he gives you the remaining portion. It might help you later down the road. After making sure that the lid is tight, put it into your plastic carton in the trunk. Remember…transmission fluid is only added by the pint. Engine oil is added by the quart. You can only use oil in the engine, and transmission fluid is used only in the transmission.

Special Note: Only add power steering fluid when power steering fluid is needed.

In the trunk you should have a plastic carton to keep all your driving goodies. Road flares are a great thing to have with you. They must be stored with care. They can break very easily. Flares do more than just warn the flow of traffic. They take the edge off of the situation, so to speak. All drivers know the meaning of the road flair. Seeing a flair up ahead means trouble. It also draws the instant attention of any police officer because of the threat to life possibilities.

Road flares must be used correctly. If you happen to come upon an accident situation and jump out of your car to help, DO NOT start a flare and go running over to the wreck like you are there to save the world. You could cause an explosion that could end your world. Pass the accident situation first, then pull over. If you pull over when you first see the accident situation, it could hamper rescue efforts. Go past the accident situation first and see if your help is needed. If you do stop to help, make sure that you pull your car over far enough to the side so when you open your driver's door it does not swing out over the right side lane marker into the flow of traffic.

It is nice to help when you can, but getting your driver's door ripped off while in the process defeats your purpose. If the door swings shut on your leg, well let's just make sure that never happens. If you cannot render effective assistance, render none at all.

No one needs someone staring at him or her asking over and over, "Are you alright?" Of course they are not alright. If they were alright then they would be standing next to you. Vocabulary is very important. The idea is not to frighten the accident victims more than they already are. The idea is to show concern with a strong feeling of control. Do not bite off more than you can chew. If you cannot help, stay out of it.

Many times I have assisted at accident scenes and was never thanked for it, but being thanked had never entered my mind. If you are looking for a big round of applause for your help, please keep going. This is not a time or place for an ego trip.

If you have a citizen band radio, call it in on channel 9. The police in many areas monitor this. If you cannot get through on this channel, then start to work up the channels asking for a "home base." A home base is just what it sounds like. It is a handle that is sitting in their home talking on the CB with a telephone close by.

A handle is a terminology used to identify the radio operator. For example, instead of using your real name, you would use something like, "Red Rider" or "The Denver Dog." You must be very careful in select social situations.

NOTE: Citizen band radios must be used correctly. If you use fowl language and get caught, expect a fine. Then, depending on the situation, do not rule out incarceration. It is not okay, use it right! Keep your contacts verbal. The voice may sound nice, just leave it as a voice.

***

You can buy prepackaged flares with the complete instructions on the back first. Then after memorizing the instructions, you can buy the cheaper flares. It is better to use the smaller packaged flares at first, for familiarization. Then purchase the larger flares.

Remember…Fire is always a threat at an accident scene.

If the fuel lines are pulled apart, the gasoline will start to leak out. If it gets to something hot enough to ignite it, your thinking goes to microseconds.

Gas from a ruptured gas tank will run off the crown in the road to the curb. Then it heads down hill to the storm drains. The vapors are the biggest threat. If they dissipate rapidly, the chance of fire is less. When you have high humidity, the gas vapors travel lower to the ground and spread out like an invisible fuse. This is the main reason you are required by law to turn the motor off at the gas station when you are pumping gas. You must also extinguish any lit or smoldering items, like pipes, cigars and cigarettes. Children should be watched closely. If you are out of the car pumping gas and the kids start playing with matches or the cigarette lighter, they can drop it out the window, causing a fire.

Remember…You must know what is going on around you at all times.

***

If you find yourself on a boat one-day and the boat operator does not turn the engine off while fueling, it is in your best interest to get out of the boat and take a walk on the dock. After the boat has been fueled and everything is secured, then you can get back into the boat. If you are on the dock and a fire starts, you can run.

If you are in the boat and a fire starts, you have a big problem. Gasoline floats on water. If it ignites and you are physically hurt from the blast, or severely burned, you may not be able to out swim the flames. Get off of the boat and onto the dock. Give yourself a chance to stretch your legs. It is a beautiful day, but it is up to you to enjoy it.

Remember…Progress can be measured in periods of time. Correcting problems in the least amount of time possible can keep a small problem from turning into a larger one. It is a take your time process. Having the right things at hand makes for progress. It is not so much being able to learn; it is what you remember that counts. Do not try to master short cuts until you have learned the long way first.

Remember…Things like extra motor oil, transmission fluid, brake fluid, windshield washer fluid, work gloves, a rag, jumper cables, a first aid kit, car wax, road flares and your own assortment of odds and ends are a must in every trunk. All of which must be kept neatly in a plastic carton of some kind.

If you have to work or walk in the rain, it will be in relative comfort if you have an umbrella. Large umbrellas go in the trunk, but you can buy one small enough to fit in your glove box. Keeping track of the things in the trunk can become a big problem if you do not have some kind of organization. You only need a carton to hold your stuff, not one to take up the entire trunk.

It is a good idea to keep some kind of loose change in the glove compartment, just in case you need to use the phone. If you call collect, the money will come back. Then with the rest of the change you can get a cup of coffee or a soda to take the edge off of the situation.

Always walk toward the best-lit area. Always walk toward the flow of traffic. I do not mean to walk head on into traffic. I mean along side of the road. If you walk down the road with your back to the flow of traffic, you will never see what hit you. Walking toward the flow of traffic gives you the opportunity to see if something is thrown at you from a passing car or maybe someone thinks it is funny to sound the car horn as they pass to scare you. Your reactions are always better when you see something coming. Maybe the driver is falling asleep behind the wheel and you're in the wrong place at the right time. The driver may not even be aware of the fact that they have left the center of the lane.

Remember…Your first and foremost responsibility is safety, and staying in the center of your lane is safety.

If your car breaks down in the middle of nowhere or on a main road, you should hang a white rag from the car's door handle to indicate distress. You must put your emergency warning lights on. If you do not know where the switch is, check the car's manual for further instructions. If you have a problem attaching the white distress signal, open the window and then close it on the corner of the rag to secure it.

Remember…Every situation is different. It's a test of your knowledge and the safety of your passengers is your first and foremost consideration in any situation.

Warning triangles are a nice idea, but they can be blown over. Even when set correctly, they do not command the attention of the flow of traffic like road flares do. If your best bet is to remain with the vehicle, get your umbrella out of the glove box or the trunk. If someone stops and starts to become aggressive, the umbrella is an excellent weapon. If you are in the car and an attacker tries to reach into the car to attack you, by opening the umbrella towards the attacker, it makes the intentions of this person very obvious for all to see. It also gives the driver time to defend themselves. The problem for the attacker is that both hands must be used to get hold of the umbrella and protect the face.

The attacker must work with arms stretched out, so as not to get poked in the face with the umbrella. This gives the driver time to locate a can of hairspray to use as a deterrent. Mace and pepper spray are excellent deterrents if the law allows. A dirty ashtray can be used or a red-hot cigarette lighter. You can throw everything that is in the glove compartment at the aggressor. With the interior lights on and screaming at the top of your lungs, if I saw this situation, I would not hesitate in going to the driver's assistance.

This general information is categorized as being "street smart." It is designed to give you a better understanding of some of the dos and don'ts of driving. Stay on the better lit roads and take your time.

***

When you jump-start a car, you must be positive that the jumper cables are connected correctly or you could cause the battery to explode. The loss of the battery is not the big problem in this situation. It is the direct threat to your face that keeps you safety minded at all times. When the top of the battery blows off, pieces of plastic fly up toward your face. The fluid in the battery is sulfuric acid and water solution. It must be washed from all areas of the skin with clean water and attended to immediately by qualified medical personnel. Do not play games with your eyes.

Do not waste time if this situation should occur. When you deal with the face, time is of the essence. When emergency personnel arrive, they are to be told exactly, I repeat, exactly what has happened.

***

What we have here are the expected mistakes and some new problems. Two of my students have never driven before. One student drove once with her father and the other must have scared the hell out of a friend. Now nobody thinks that she will ever drive. She openly agrees with her friends, this situation will call for more attention. This could be a peer pressure thing. If so, it has to be nipped in the bud.

They both have a good attitude and that is what is all about. Another driver did not sit too tall in the saddle, so to speak. I asked her if she wanted the phone book from the trunk and she got mad. Now we are driving down the road with her telling me that she can see just fine and that I should not worry.

I am not to worry means Red Alert. The student that tells me not to worry straightens me right up in the seat. I love a good challenge and this attitude shows me that I may have a very overconfident driver or an excellent sense of humor on my hands. Either one can get you into trouble. "Can you see?" I asked her. "Oh yes I can see fine, thank you," she said. This student shows great ability but sits too low in the seat.

This all becomes more and more interesting as we go along. Next, what we have to do is a work up on each student. This way we can find the areas that need the most attention. My system of using visual aids to enhance the awareness of your surroundings makes short work of blind spot problems.

Remaining in the center of the lane is easier because you are more comfortable with the feeling of control. Confidence and control go hand in hand.

I am starting to feel like mister answer man. The first few weeks seem to be taken up correcting bad habits and giving countless explanations that should have been understood by the new driver long ago. Teaching a person to drive well enough to pass the road test is wrong. The idea of "killing an hour" is wrong. If you do not take driving seriously, you should not be an instructor.

There are excellent driving instruction to be had. There are well-established driving schools in all areas that cater directly to teenage misinterpretation. I have students that passed the road test and cannot change lanes. Lane changing should be part of all road tests.

* Remember…that the proper use of directionals while operating a motorized vehicle is required by law. That means that there were so many people not going along with the system at the time that the courts felt it was in the interest of safety, and safety is a key word here concerning the general public, and made it a law. I would think it is a carry over idea from the horse and carriage days, where signaling for change of directions or intent had to be done with hand signals and eye contact. There's that eye contact again.

***

Today a student drove around a parked car. He had to go over the double line onto the other side of the road in the process. You must always be prepared for a situation like this. You must be prepared to stop in case something is coming toward you on the oncoming side of the road. Never challenge right of way. If you see that the car approaching is closer to the object than you are, even odds the driver of the approaching car will pick up speed to try to get by first. Always work with a B type personality and directionals. For a B type personality, the idea is to concentrate on keeping peace in your surroundings. An A type personality is living in a false world of security. From my personal experiences, you never know what to expect. That is the big challenge to driving. Take your time; try to memorize your surroundings.

***

Having work gloves in the trunk is a good idea. You can change a flat tire and not even get your hands dirty. Make sure the gloves fit your hands well. If the gloves are super big, they will get in the way and could cause a problem.

When you are checking under the hood, keep your hands back where you can see them. If you are showing off and put your hand too close to the moving belts, it could cost you a finger. If you see someone with a rag in their hand working on the motor and it is running, check to see if the rag is hanging down towards the belts. If this is the case, do not call to the person to move it. Instead, walk over calmly and move the rag back out of harms way, if it is safe to do so. Then explain your actions. If you call to the person, they may turn towards you to see what you want and drop the rag down further, causing it to get caught in the belts. There is a right and a wrong way to help. Always remember that nobody likes to be corrected and when it comes to driving, everyone is always correct.

***

My students are asking a lot of questions about jump starting a car, so, let's go back to it for a moment. Jump starting a car is not something to be trifled with. When you buy a car, ask the seller to show you the best advised procedure for that particular model car. The jumper cables are color-coded. The positive is the red and the negative is black. You must be positive that the red goes to the red and the black goes to the black. If you connect them to the wrong terminals, it could cause battery damage.

Remember…If the cables are connected wrong, it could cause damage to the electrical system of the car giving the jump.

Connect the red to red on one car then connect the red to the red on the other car. Then connect the black to black on the car giving the jump first. With the black or negative clamp in hand, try to clamp it onto metal first. The idea of this is to lessen the chance of an explosion. If you have an aluminum block, the electrical contact must be made in a different location. If no good surface is to be found, the negative clamp is to be placed onto the battery post directly.

This is done by checking exactly where the clamp is to go, then squeeze the clamp open, holding it at arms length with your face away, connect the cable by watching out of the corner of your eye. Working in this fashion lessens the chance of facial lacerations, should the battery decide to explode. Do not connect cables to anything that will move when the motor starts. Never connect cables to metal fan blades.

With the cables in place, start the car you are jumping from and let it run for a short time before trying to start the car being jumped. If you chose to leave the car you are jumping from running, you must take even more care in hooking up the jumper cables.

The car battery produces an explosive gas that can collect around the battery vents. The spark that occurs increases the chance of an explosion.

The humidity factor plays a big part in the battery exploding. When the humidity is low, the gasses dissipate more rapidly. When the humidity is high, the gases tend to stay closer to the ground. In this case it would be the top of the battery. This increases the chances of the top blowing off when the last connection is made. Ask your parents to show you how it is done.

Remember…Do not be afraid to ask. It could make life much easier for you one day, somewhere down the road.

When you turn the key, if the car tries to start and almost does, but then slows down or stops, turn the key off and wait another minute or so before trying to start the car again.

After the car starts, "Do Not Race The Engine." The motor will run a bit faster by itself. Just because the motor is running, this Is No Reason To Drop Your Guard. You are now working under the hood with a running motor and Extreme Care Must Be Taken when removing the jumper cables. With arms stretched and face turned as much away from the battery as possible, remove the black or ground cable from the car being jumped first. Then remove the black or ground cable from the car giving the jump. Then remove the red or positive cable from the now started car.

Last but not least, remove the red to red connection from the car giving the jump. Cables are removed in reverse order. If you are doing this by yourself, you must make sure that the cables do not hang down into the engine compartment and get tangled up with the now moving belts. Make sure that the ends of the jumper cables never touch each other. This will create a spark and scare you half to death.

Remember…Common sense dictates that if you have a standard shift and the parking brake does not work, it may be better advised to keep your foot on the brake pedal to keep the car from moving. Every situation is different; you have to figure out the safest way to do things.

Ask someone who makes sense to go over it with you, in a hands on situation. This is something you should be able to do safely and without hesitation. After the car has been started and everything is removed from the engine compartment, don't forget To Put Your things Back into the Trunk. The car should sit for a few minutes before you try to drive; this allows the battery time to charge up. Even then, it should be driven to a safe haven. The next time you turn the motor off it might not start again.

Just because you borrowed the car and the battery died, does not mean that it's your fault. They don't last forever, approximately four, maybe six years at the most. But, if you jump start a car and something goes wrong with the battery or the alternator because of an error on your behalf, Restitution is to be expected. Batteries are like anything else, if you buy cheap you get cheap. When it's time to buy a battery, it pays to buy a good one. Always keep the guarantee.

Color codes tell you where wires go. Red or positive is called the hot wire and must never make direct contact with the black or negative wire. This we refer to as the Ground wire. To make it easier, we refer to it as live and ground. The two make contact in controlled situations throughout the car, creating a comfortable lighting system and supporting the onboard computer. When you jump start a car, the key must be turned off while the cables are being connected. There are fuses throughout the system to prevent fire if a system were to short out. The fuse will burn out first instead of the wires. If you add something to the car, it must have a fuse. For example, some replacement radios have a fuse on the back of the radio. This is a great idea. Sometimes people take short cuts during installation and the short cut is usually to leave out the fuse. "Bad Idea."

If you let the red handled end of the jumper cables touch any metal surface after it's connected to the battery, it will cause a spark. If the black handled cable touches metal, it will cause a small spark if something in the car is on. Whereas, the red to ground combination will create a larger spark.

Make sure all switches, including radio and heat, are turned off before trying to jumpstart the car. With a jumpstart situation, you even keep your foot off the brake when you're starting the car, so you get all the electricity you can down to the starter motor. Make sure the emergency brake or parking brake is on. This will keep the car from rolling. With a standard shift transmission, the car should be in neutral with clutch pedal pressed to the mat. If you turn the key and the car shows any kind of forward or reverse motion, press the brake pedal down hard to stop the motion. Turn the key off immediately. Remove the key from the ignition and find out where your mistake is.

Wow, that was some great stuff. It is up to you to get a better idea of the subject material by reading it twice.

Please Remember that you must ask an adult how to do something before you attempt it alone. Even with your good friends, you may still be alone.

Never touch a car without permission.

You will become a better informed driver as you go along. It takes approximately two years of driving time before you get good. That's two years of driving time, not two years of your life.

Remember…It takes a while to get good at all of the different aspects of driving.

Chapter 2

STUDENT COMMENTS

Mr. Myers,

I started Driver's Ed. only a few weeks after I got my driver's license and I found the driving sessions to be helpful in acquiring the basics of my driving skills. I think that you most taught me to use the rear view mirror. I also gained a better course of direction within the general area because of our often-long journeys to far off places. I have increased my awareness of the other drivers and have been able to identify subtleties of other drivers and their driving abilities.

***

Driver's Education with Mr. Myers has taught me many ways to handle my car better, thus making my driving experience a safer one. For example, I learned to use my inside mirror to check for cars and potential accidents behind me. I also feel I have improved my gas mileage. I now get more miles out of a gas tank than I used to before Driver's Ed.

***

The most important thing that I gained from Driver's Ed. was the ability to utilize the mirror correctly. I developed the habit of checking the inside mirror when I slow down and stop.

In addition to that, I learned important things about wheel control and adjusting speed to road conditions. Have a good summer.

***

I feel okay when I start out driving but once I see my first violation, I start getting a bit angry. I guess I get really angry because I take the other people's driving violations as a personal cheap shot against me. I feel comfortable about driving, but not about other drivers.

***

I've learned the hand over hand maneuver.
I've learned to check my mirror often when I brake.
I've learned how to deal with skidding.
I've learned to drive defensively and watch out for other people's stupid mistakes.

***

I learned a lot about steering and using all aspects of driving in general. Many key aspects were hand over hand recovery, brake control, and using the mirror in many cases. I learned how to have control over mileage by cruising down hills, letting the car settle down at the tops of hills, stopping at signs and lights, using my eyes to watch everything around, checking blind spots, and looking at intersections thoroughly.

***

Most cars today are designed to start without touching the gas. If you have to pump the gas pedal every time you start the car, there is something desperately wrong. With an older car, I can see tapping the gas lightly only once in the morning to insure a smooth start, but if you have to tap the gas pedal all the time to get it going, something is wrong.

As the car sits overnight the oil drains into the oil pan. I check the oil in the morning. When you first start the car, the oil rings on the pistons are not filled completely with oil. They may not make a good seal against the cylinder walls the first few time that the pistons go up and down. The oil pump is the heart of motor. Checking and changing the oil is very important.

Fuel injected cars might have a computer controlled cold start system. This mixes extra gas to insure a successful start. Your system might have what is called an automatic choke. This does the toe tapping for you.

With a diesel motor you have a glow plug. The glow plug raises the temperature in the intake manifold to insure first starts in foul weather. The switch or button must be in the "On" position until the indicator light goes out before starting. Read the Owner's Manual. If the system is automatic, you must not try to start the car until the indicator buzzer goes off or the indicator light goes out.

Remember…everything electrical must be turned off in the car before you start it. Check the radio and heater fan. Make sure they are off.

A manual choke is the black knob with the word "choke" in white printed letters. The word choke may be on the dashboard; if so, it will probably be more ornate. If you have this system, you must check the "Owner's Manual" for directions. You have to know how far to pull the choke out. With some cars you only need to pull the choke out half way. You may have to pull it all the way out. You won't know until you ask.

After the car starts, you have to push the choke back in. This is an art. It must be pushed back in slowly as the motor starts to run smoothly. The big problem is the amount of raw fuel that's burnt. It leaves carbon deposits on the top of the pistons. After a while, hot spots could develop on the top of the pistons. This is a piece of carbon that can stay hot enough to act like a spark plug. A spark plug sets off a gaseous mixture in the cylinder when the piston comes up on the compression stroke. This action is well controlled, but post ignition can be a problem. If you turn the key off and strange noises come out from under the hood, it could very well be a post ignition situation.

If you turn the key off and the motor doesn't seem like it wants to stop, turn the key back on. If the motor starts to run smoothly again, this is post ignition. In this situation, turning the key back on means just that. You do not turn the key into the spring-loaded area like you do when you start a car. You turn the key only to the on position. Let the car run for a moment or so, then turn it off again.

If you have this problem, try changing to the highest-octane gas you can buy. After five fill ups or so, it should start to clear up. Check your local auto parts store, they might have something you can add to the gas that may help fix the problem.

***

Windshield washer fluid is sold in one-gallon containers and is added directly to the windshield washer reserve tank, located somewhere under the hood. Check the manual for the location or go to someone who makes sense and ask him or her to show you where to put it in.

If purchased in smaller containers, it will be concentrated. This means you add the windshield washer fluid, then clean water. When you add water, it must be clean water. Contaminates will cause streaks on the glass. Be sure you read the instructions on the container first, so you add the right amount of water.

Remember…if you add the wrong thing, you must get it out. Tell your parents right away, straighten it out immediately. Don't play games.

I check the container the washer fluid comes in. If it's a clear container, and the color is blue, I'll buy it. If it's in a plastic container and I can't see the color, I check it out further.

Buying the gallon container at the checkout when you go food shopping is an excellent money saver. Put it in your plastic carton.

Most drivers, of which you are one, do not get the full wear out of their windshield wiper blades, and do not even know it. If you keep the windshield clean and the wiper blades clean, the blades will last twice as long. The blades should be cleaned with soap and water.

On most cars they are out of sight; this makes it much easier just to take it for granted that they work properly. As the operator of a motorized vehicle, you can never take anything for granted.

I saw a driver cleaning the wiper blades with gasoline. This is not a smart thing to do. This softens the rubber and will cause very bad streaking. They must be cleaned with a mild abrasive, like soap and water.

When you buy new wiper blades, take the old blades and put them into the box the new blades came out of and put them in your carton in your trunk. If, somewhere down the road, you lose one, you can replace it on the spot. If you lose a blade, the wiper arm can scratch the windshield. This could cost you the price of a replacement windshield. That's expensive.

It also makes it easier to buy new blades. You just walk into your local parts store with the box and match up the numbers. You only need to keep one extra set. You do not want to start a collection of wiper blades. When you change your wiper blades, throw out the set in the trunk, and keep what you just took off.

***

Please be very careful jump-starting your car. The live must never touch any metal. Always keep things where you can see them; never pull jumper cables off. You clamped it on, so you unclamp it. Plastic goggles are nice to have on hand for this occasion. So…red is positive and is shown with the Plus sign. We call it live. Ground is negative and is identified by the color Black, or a minus sign. I just thought I'd throw that in.

***

I like general information. It can cover anything. So, we might as well go to car waxes and compounds. When you are finished using them, make sure the tops or lids are on tight before putting them back into the plastic carton. Compound is used to clean the surface and wax seals the surface, leaving it smooth and shiny.

When the paint's finish starts to break down, it's called oxidation. Compound cleans off this oxidation. Red compound is used with the rougher surfaces; white compound is used to bring out an even shine. Using a buffing machine takes practice.

If you use Red compound on old paint, you could burn through the paint. That means you just buffed through the paint and are looking at the primer coat. The primer coat of paint is between the metal surface and the paint. Use white compound; it cleans great and it is easy to wipe off or wash off. **Never wax your car in the sun**. Big problems.

Remember…Always ask a move knowledgeable person before cleaning with compounds.

You remove road tar with a little bit of diesel fuel, or something from the parts store. They have it; you just have to ask. You cannot remove road tar with compound. If you do, it will take off more paint than it will tar. Use tar remover first, and then go over the area with wax. Liquid wax is easy and fast. Always use a circular motion. Straight back and forth motions leave streaks in the paint that may be hard to get out. If by chance you make a mistake and need to have it buffed out; it might be in your best interest to take it to a place where they clean the entire car from head to toe. They buff the car and clean the interior. Not like running a vacuum hose across it quick trying to do everything before your time runs out, it's cleaned like you would clean it, if you had the time and interest.

The one thing that you should always find time for is, "Making a Good Impression." You will learn that the people driving clean cars seem to be paying more attention to what's going on around them.

When you sell your car, you want to get what it is worth, right? Well if you are involved in an accident, the insurance adjuster will determine the value of the car. Its age and its condition determine a car's value: condition being the way the car has been maintained.

For example…if the book value is $6,000 in good condition, it can be worth thousands less in bad condition. A car supplies transportation and is also an investment.

Do not wax the windshield of your car; it will cause glare and streaking. If you have liquid wax put on your car at the car wash, make sure the attendants clean it off the windshield. If they tell you it's OK, I myself would question the use of liquid wax at all. Maybe I can save some more money. These little things in the long run can save a lot of money.

***

A first aid kit is a good item to have if used correctly. We must go by past actions taken against people who only stopped to help and then found themselves in the courtroom explaining their actions. When the first aid kit comes out, needless to say every situation is different; you must use your common sense. Our hearts go out to the people who are hurt, but you can't let your heart over-ride your common sense or you won't be of any use at all. You will only get in the way. Don't play with what you don't know.

Talking to a person can be very relaxing. It helps the time go faster. If the person is in shock, they can still hear you; they just lack at that moment the ability to respond. So you do all the talking. Talk about anything. When you talk to the person, you do not scream.

Remember…if you are affected by the situation, the person will pick it up right away in your voice.

***

Picking an area of interest when it comes to driving is easy. Trying to keep them in proper sequence does become a problem. The reason is, when you talk about driving, there are so many different aspects that the conversation could go from tires to dashboards. You should never put anything on your dashboard that makes it shine, it creates a glare on the windshield. One minute, one person has the floor and the next minute, everybody is listening to your ideas about tire maintenance.

Later we will be talking about conditioned reflexes. These are the things that keep you out of trouble. The faster your reactions are, the less trouble you are likely to get into.

Let's get a broader idea of safety. The road has a crown. This is the name given to the center of the road. The center of the road is higher than the sides. This allows the rain to wash dirt off the road over to the curbs. This is what the street cleaners are cleaning up when they sweep the streets. Storm drains have catch buckets or a wire mesh screen to catch larger items. After entering the storm drain, the water finds its way out to sea. The construction of a road is very interesting. There is a lot more that goes into the construction than meets the eye.

Your first and foremost responsibility is to stay in the center of your lane. We need a place to start and this is it. Because the center of the road is higher, we must be constantly checking to make sure that the car does not start to drift off toward the right side of the road. You must keep a good grip on the wheel, just in case.

If you were to start to fall asleep behind the wheel, because your mind is programmed to see the car in the center, we hope the reaction would be to spring back to life before a crash. You know the feelings of your hands on the wheel. If you felt one hand becoming loose and dropping down on the wheel, this would also bring you back to life. You must train yourself or this can become a big problem. Just because we know what we know doesn't mean we know it all. If you get back to the center of the lane and your foot moves from the gas to the brake at the same time, this is a conditioned reflex.

We do not want to have accidents. In an accident situation, your common sense dictates that you are to take the lesser of two evils.

If my driver's door gets hit, the force of the impact is directed directly to me. If the impact is to the right side of the car, the chances of physical damage to the driver is lessened. If the steering wheel is on the right side of the car then that door is your main concern.

Remember…you can always get another car. In an accident situation, the value of the car must become zero. If you start to think, "Oh, my fender", or "Oh, my door," you'll forget about the most important thing in the car. The most important thing is your safety and the safety of your passengers.

If you were to drift toward the center of the road and go running into the oncoming flow of traffic, the smell of death is very present. You could drift over and kill someone on the other side of the road. We have a thing called a mystery accident. This is when the car goes off the road for no apparent reason, in good weather conditions. There is no sign of foul play. No drug or alcohol misuse is in the picture.

If you drift to the side, you could hit a parked car or a mailbox. Maybe even hit a telephone pole. You might drive into a ditch. If you drift off the road, anything you could hit could kill you or you could kill anything you hit.

*****

It's the simple things that we miss, and it's the simple things that open the door for big mistakes. If you feel drowsy, open your window and get some fresh air. That's just the start. Now you have to figure out what is causing drowsiness. The first thing you check is the heater. If the heater vents are aimed at you, the heat from the heater is coming directly into your face. This will put you to sleep in no time.

Heat is sneaky. At first you feel warm and comfortable, then you start to become drowsy. This can come over you slowly or very rapidly; it depends on your physical condition. If you get behind the wheel and you are tired, the chances of you having an accident are excellent. The longer the trip, the greater the chance of falling asleep behind the wheel. If you have only driven for short distance on the roads in your general area, you are not ready for a long trip. You have to start with small distances first. This builds up your resistance. Yes, you could attempt a long distance run and have no problem getting there; it's the getting home part that will get you. When you are going somewhere new, your point of concentration is very strong. On the way back at night, it's different.

This is the anxiety factor. When you travel towards a new destination, your eyes are open wide so that you won't miss anything.

On your way back, you know where you're going. You have it very clear in your mind. No big problem, but it's usually at night. So, long trips should be taken in daylight as much as possible.

If you feel yourself becoming drowsy, open the window and re-direct the heat. You could turn it down or maybe turn it off completely for awhile. You could cut back on the heat and leave the fan on high, but the window is opened first whenever there is any sign of drowsiness.

Turn the radio to a country and western station and sing out loud to the best of your ability. Change the words around to fit your situation. You need to realize the real danger here.

Sit up straight in the driver's seat and re-adjust your inside mirror. Pick up something and tell yourself out loud all about the object. Maybe something out of the glove compartment would help. If you cannot reach the glove box, this is no time to try. Have your passengers open their windows. Read all the gauges and tell yourself what they mean, anything to wake you up. When you sing along, it increases the oxygen in your body. If you really get involved, it gets your adrenaline gland going. The adrenaline wakes you up, helping you to find a safe place to stop.

The combination of adrenaline and oxygen act like a cup of coffee, but it does not last long. Sometimes the drowsy feeling can come on very fast and you may not catch yourself actually falling asleep.

Don't fool yourself into thinking that you can make it those last few miles. Any experienced driver will tell you the same thing.

If you have to stop, you have to stop. It's not wrong to stop. It's wrong to push yourself. The time it takes to make the trip can never be put before your safety. You can never compromise the safety factor.

Stay in the lit areas. Find a gas station and get something to drink. Check your gas gauge again just to be really sure it's what you believe it to be. Stranger things have happened. The next gas station may be more than a few miles down the road.

If you stop to get a cup of coffee and gas and the attendant wants to put in oil, get out and check it yourself. If you find yourself in a situation where the attendant's personality is, to say the least, overpowering, and you sense deception, get him out from under the hood. Check to make sure everything is in place and shut the hood. It's your car. You have to protect your investment. But, if someone pulls a gun on you, it's not the time to argue.

***

If you find yourself having to put your bright lights on all the time in order to see better, your headlights may be dirty, or you might be driving to fast. If you take a trip and stop for gas, turn the lights out. Wash the brake lights and the headlights. You may be very surprised at the difference.

The lighting system on your car is your responsibility, If a bulb burns out, you must fix it right away. I was stopped one night for a taillight. I carry my own collection of extra things, one of which is an extra brake light bulb. I changed the bulb right on the spot and did not get a ticket. You drive most of the time in a limited area and the local police get used to seeing certain cars. If you can correct a problem on the spot, the next time the officer sees you, the officer may see you more in the light of an attentive driver, rather than some sort of hell-bent teenager. Think about it: if five cars are going down the road and one is driven by a teenager, who's going to get pulled over?

You have to know where the light switch is in your car. If you borrow a car, make sure the owner of the car shows you how to work the lights. The last thing in the world you need is it to get dark and not be able to find the light switch. It's your responsibility as the operator of the motorized vehicle to be fully aware of the functions and locations of all switches, levers, pedals, handles and knobs.

Some cars have a pull out and push in switch, out turns the lights on, in turns them off. Another style is mounted on the steering column and is twisted to turn the lights on and off. It could consist of two or more levers mounted on either side of the steering wheel.

Your best bet is to locate the manual that came with the car for best results. That's why it came with the car.

Pulling or twisting to the first notch puts your parking lights on. In this position, all the lights except the headlights come on. Depending on the switch, pull or twist again and the headlights come on. If you put your lights on and the interior lights come on, don't get bent out of shape. If it's a pull out type switch, turn the knob and the interior lights should go out. If you continue to turn it, it will turn down the dashboard lights. Again, it's best to have your parents go over it with you. This is not something you can say you know until you prove to yourself that you do.

Please understand that in no way am I insinuating that you are a bad driver. I am just saying that you are a new driver and we all learn at our own pace. Getting behind the wheel requires patience and when things become confusing, we have the tendency to lose patience with ourselves.

The bright light switch is lifted up towards you and then released. On most models, it is usually the directional lever. If a blue light comes on the dashboard when you lift the lever towards you and let it go, the light means your bright lights are on. If you lift it towards you again and let it go, the bright lights go out. Practice makes perfect. Check the owners manual.

***

It snowed today, so we didn't have any driving. Snow can cover up bigger problems on the road. You know about the accumulation of oil in the center of the lane. It's the darkened center of the lane. It is caused by cars leaking oil and stays in place because the tires on your car are rolling to the left and right of it. When you change lanes, your tires must cross over it coming out of the lane and must cross over it again going into the next. Take your time. As the weather just keeps weathering, a build up of snow will form over the oil-laden area. With this snow and slush in the center of the lane, changing lanes may not be a good idea. Stay in the tracks that the other cars have made through the snow as much as possible.

Remember…keep your speed down; watch your wheel control. Always leave enough distance in case you have to slide to a safe stop.

If you must cross over into another lane, first make sure you have enough speed to cross over the snow or slush accumulation. At one point you could have all four tires pushing through the snow or slush. This is the main reason you never change lanes in a turn in bad weather. Try not to change lanes in a turn at all. If you can see the tracks from another car that has changed lanes, use those tracks instead of making new ones. If you allow the wheels to drift into the snow it could cause you to lose control of the car. You must keep your tires rolling on the clearest and cleanest part of the road at all times.

You have to use your directional and check your inside mirror and blind spot to make sure that if something were to go wrong, that no one else would be involved but you. We read all about how to control a car in a skid, but you can't really know about skidding unless you have experienced the sensation.

Remember…the front wheel drive car is not the miracle worker in the snow that it is cracked up to be. Attitude, judgement, and control will see you through.

As you cross over the mid-lane accumulation of snow or slush, it might be in your best interest to ease up off the gas just a bit. This lets the weight of the car push down on the front wheels more. You will feel the tires making their way through the snow. This will slow the car down some and allow you to get a better feel of the wheel. If you apply the brake, be careful not to lock your wheels up. With all the ups and downs involved, you can better understand that the worse the weather gets, the less lane changing you do.

People get stupid when it snows. They think that nothing has changed and try to drive in the snow just like they drive on clear roads. No can do. So, if at all possible, do not drive in the snow until the roads have been cleared. If you have to drive in snowy conditions, you must always leave more than enough time for your trip, in case you are delayed by another driver's misfortune. Take your time and keep your speed down.

Stopping to help someone who has managed to get themselves stuck in the snow is a nice idea as long as you don't get stuck in the snow yourself when you pull over to help.

Pulling a car out of the snow can damage your car. If it's your own car, then it's up to you. But, if its your parents' car, then you have no place in the picture to be hooking up to a car to try to pull or push it anywhere. Unless you have direct permission from the owner, or have been given permission by your parents, you do nothing but drive it and check the proper items to keep the car operational.

Let's say your friend gets stuck in a snowdrift and you call home to get permission to help. Now whoever you talk to is doing something else at the time and doesn't really understand the problem. You take the OK as permission to do so and hook a chain between the two cars and start to pull. If you damage the car in any way, who do you think is going to take the weight from Mom and Dad? Parents are good people, give them a break.

***

One student came to class today with a teenager know-it-all attitude, but it seems to be a front. I wont have a problem if this is the case. Another student may get tired of practicing left and right turns and decide to come down to earth. If not, it's off to the office we go. I will not let a show off attitude affect another student's progress. It's like a puppy; if you let it go it could run into the road and get killed, or cause a major accident. So you must train it with a leash first. In this case, I have to slow him down. Tunnel vision also seems to be a problem.

Remember…speed and tunnel vision go hand in hand. If you have one problem, the other is present. You have to think closer to you for your peripheral vision to stay open.

One student who commented last week that she thought she knew how to drive, walked away saying to her friends, "I drove good today, didn't I?" Her friends were agreeing with her, except for the stop lines.

The ear to ear smile, the tone of voice, the air of accomplishment, this is a positive sign of self-confidence.

With another student, I started to open her vision by having her turn her head-first to the left then back to the road in front of the car. I asked her what she saw. She told me she saw a house, I asked her to tell me what color the front door was. She told me white. Then I asked her what number was on the front door and she knew the number without checking. After a few more practice glances to the right side, I pointed out to her that her speed had dropped ten miles per hour. Everyone in the car was impressed.

This student shows great promise; she is listening to what I'm saying and trying to see what I'm seeing. All of my students have this ability. Some have to break through a social shell of some sort. Others will fall into place like clockwork.

These exercises are all planned ahead of time. I pick a house with no bushes or trees to block the view. I wait until the driver's door is almost straight across from the house door, then have the driver glance once to the left and then bring the eyes back to the road in front of the car.

It can be considered a set-up that works. I think its called creativity; I like genius. Getting a driver to relax behind the wheel is the start of self-confidence. Memorizing objects also builds self-confidence. You relax and your speed drops down to your personal pace. You must find your own pace first, then build from there.

Conditioned reflexes will fall into place if you practice. One student pulled away from the curb and did not use her directional. After we had gotten going, I asked her why she didn't give the required signal of intent. She told me that she had checked it and it was clear so there was no reason to use the directional. When I told her that she was wrong and that she was leaving herself open to get hit in her driver's door, she said that she didn't have to use the directional if there was nothing there. Well, let me tell you what I told her. You are required by law to use your directional, not when you want, but all the time.

Remember…If another driver sees your directional they may sound their horn and an accident may be avoided.

I asked her if she ever tied her sneakers and had to retie them a few minutes later. She answered yes. I asked her if she had ever tried to open a door to find it locked. She answered yes. Then I asked her if she had ever been scared by a loud sound that made her jump. She answered yes.

She started to get the idea. We are human and make mistakes. If there is nothing there the first time you check, you tell yourself there will be something there the second time you check. Never drop your guard. The one time you take it for granted that it's clear to go, it won't be.

.   ***

Today I'm going to ask my students to drive to the best of their ability. As I watch every move they make. I take notes on the students driving ability and general behavior. If I start to write a lot of things down, the students get real nervous. If I make a casual mark in my book, the students tend to be more relaxed. The student will ask what was done wrong. I tell them that I have to add everything up to get my answer. I tell them to watch the way they drive and see what problems they can find, then we will match observations at the end of the driving session. If it needed to be corrected, I would have corrected it on the spot.

Rather than going through a twenty-minute explanation, it's much more productive when you get the students to study themselves. It's hard to know what a person is thinking. If you can get a student to ask a question, I know that after I give my answer, the student's mind will remain open to driving. In the same respect, I am well known for my twenty-minute explanation ability. Each student is different and it takes a few weeks to figure them out.

I have two students with bad cases of tunnel vision. They both understand what it is and can tell me all about it, but can't see it in themselves. You must be properly introduced to a motor vehicle.

The worst thing that you can do is to put a new driver behind the wheel without first taking the new driver under your wing, so to speak. Parents have the responsibility to take the time and explain to the new driver different situations that they have gone through, and express the fear of the moment. Learning how to do something the hard way is the wrong way.

***

From talking with my students, I have noticed a pattern of sorts when it comes to getting traffic tickets. In one situation, a driver was having a problem putting in a CD. This is called dropping your guard. He allowed himself to be distracted and lost the center of the lane. He was concentrating more on the radio than his driving. This plus slowing down at the same time made him stand out like a sore thumb.

He might have even used the brake during his dilemma; anyway this is all happening on a parkway, so I was told. If you have a problem, it is in the best interest of all involved to pull over at the first safe haven and take care of it. Drifting back and forth in the lane is a sign of intoxication and no police officer will pass up the chance to arrest a drunk driver. This abnormal driving behavior falls under the heading of probable cause. The driver was pulled over and given two tickets. One for the control factor and the other for abnormal car activity.

Can you visualize how this car must have looked going down the highway drifting back and forth in the lane with the brake lights going on and off? It's no wonder he was pulled over. If you don't think about your actions, all sorts of situations will pop up.

If you pay attention and something happens, your chances of avoiding contact with another object is greater. If you see it coming you can make some kind of adjustment. If you don't see it coming, you're going to take a beating. You are not a bad driver; you are a new driver and must watch to make sure you don't drop your guard. If you must, for any reason, travel at a low rate of speed in any traffic situation, it is required by law that you put on your four way flashers to warn the flow of traffic of impending danger.

The worst is to check your mirror to find a police car behind you with the lights on telling you to pull over. What can you say in your defense when you don't know what you did wrong? This is a humiliating situation, to say the least. The outcome was that one ticket was dropped, that was the in the car activity; the other ticket for control had to be paid. This put points on the driver's license and because of the probation period, the driver might just have his driving privileges suspended for a while.

The policeman did his job by giving two tickets and showing up in court. What the driver did was wrong, but to what degree? If this had happened during rush hour traffic, it could have caused a major accident. When you talk about major accidents, you're usually talking death.

Further education in the subject of driving is a must. There is no way you can pass a road test and then think you can just come out here and drive. Passing a road test means you have met the minimum requirements; there is always something to learn about driving. Another item has materialized, this being that if you don't go to court, the ticket will somehow go away. Nice try but no cigar. The court can send you an invitation that you just can't refuse. If you get a ticket, take care of it right away.

Tell your parents about it before they get a letter from their insurance company telling them that their insurance rates have gone up. Anyone can make a mistake. There are classes you can take to lower your insurance rates and take points off of your license. Getting a ticket is like all of us telling one person that their actions on the road need to be reconsidered.

***

Let's get back to the diary. A teacher tries to teach and the student tries to learn. After the ice is broken, the true personalities of the students emerge.

Let's get an idea of what your up against by selecting one of my students, find the mistakes, then you match them up to yours. You have to do that part. So...let's go. Wheel control, the inside or rear view mirror is not used correctly at all. Directionals are not used correctly at all; checking the outside mirror leaving the curb. That's a big mistake. As far as the blind spot goes, this student can't even point to them. Excess braking, rolling after stops, California rolling stops, stops over stop line, turns onto the roads going over the end of a stop line, I have a comment on this one. When you make a turn, you must make sure that you turn into the center of your lane.

Remember...the one spot you never want to get hit is your driver's door. When you make your turns, you must be right on the money every time.

Now, back to class, tunnel vision, gear selection problems, lane change, speed, observation, judgement and control, attitude and spaz.

Nerves seem to be a big factor. This student has passed the road test and thinks he is doing well. The problem is that once you pass the road test, most of the time you drive by yourself, so you make excuses to yourself for your mistakes. The idea is not to learn by hitting things.

When you find your pace, you will find that you have more time to check things out as you drive. Because you are calm, you not only see more, but you understand more. If you are a new driver, there is no way you can keep up with the flow of traffic safely. This is a new class and I always have a few students who know more than I do. I try to straighten that out right off the bat. But, there is always one who just doesn't seem to get the message.

The student, whose mistakes were listed above, was driving down the road not paying attention to the posted speed limit. I told him to slow down, but he wouldn't. I had already told him that if he got a ticket in the driving portion of driver's ed., he would be dropped from the course. Then, out of the clear blue sky, a student in the back seat told the driver to slow down. This is what I like to see. The student told the driver to stop playing the role of the fool and think of the passenger's safety. The safety of the passengers is the driver's responsibility. Another back seat driver added that if he didn't slow down that he would be responsible for his safety when we switched drivers. He slowed down.

***

We are in the colder months of the year and there is snow on the side's of the road. You have to memorize the icy areas by you. When you get fresh snow, it covers the ice on the roads. You may see the new snow and forget about the ice underneath. I could get into the, "its too late part" but I would prefer to talk about options you have when you start to lose control. First off, when you start to slide because you pressed the brake too hard and too fast, ease off the brake enough to let the wheels turn again. Don't freak out. That's easy to say, but when it's happening, it is a different story. I don't care how many years of experience you have, when you first start to slide, it will spook you.

Remember…because of the crown in the road, you may start to slide off to one side of the road or the other. We have a natural tendency to automatically turn the wheel in the opposite direction of the skid. When you let the wheels turn again; the car will go in the direction the wheels are turned. This change of direction may give you enough control to avoid an accident.

***

The news just had a story about some ice that fell off the top of a tractor-trailer and came down on the car behind it. The ice broke the windshield and cut the lady driver up pretty good. It took stitches to put her face back together. This is a big common sense item. There is a law that you have to remove large amounts of snow from your car before you enter the flow of traffic. You're responsible for the damage. If you are driving a long distance in the snow, you have to stop whenever necessary to clean the accumulation of snow off your car. If the snow comes off the hood and onto your windshield, it could cause you to drive off the road.

This is what we mean by common sense. You see it could be a problem, so you take care of it before it becomes a problem. Here is a tip on how to start your car in the cold weather. If the motor seems to be turning over a little slower because of the cold, you should press in the clutch; so the gears in the transmission will not turn. When you start the car in neutral, the gear oil in the standard transmission could be thicker than motor oil and when it gets cold, it gets real thick. When you press the clutch in, it allows the starter motor to turn just the motor and makes for faster starts.

If you have heavy weight oil in the motor, it will cause hard starting in the cold weather. Keep your foot on the clutch after the motor has started until it starts to run smoothly. Then you ease up on the clutch pedal slowly so that the stirring of the cold gear oil doesn't stall the motor. Please make sure its in neutral.

***

Different things stand out on different days. Today was a 4x4 day. A 4x4 is designed for off-road and must be watched very, very carefully when driven on normal roads. Inexperienced drivers do not respect the power that a 4x4 vehicle has. One student was leaving the parking lot with a 4-wheel drive vehicle in 4-wheel drive. He gave it gas like you would give a car to get going. To his surprise, the wagon took off straight across the road.

The driver was able to regain control, but not before going up on a lawn, and hitting a good-sized tree and stone wall. I could see into the wagon as they drove past me, and all the people in the wagon were noticeably shaken. I had a chance to talk with the driver later on. I told him he was lucky, and he agreed with that. I told him that I knew what he did wrong. It was in 4-wheel drive, right? He said yes. I asked him if he had it in low range. He answered yes. The radio was on, right? He said yes. Trying to impress somebody, right? He started to laugh; he won't do that again. He was lucky this time, he only bent up the license plate.

***

You are driving down the road with your eyes wide open, understanding the importance of your surroundings , traveling within your pace, relaxed with the feeling of responsibility and control.

You wind up at a stop sign. As the car stops, you are checking your mirror, just to be sure that you are not going to get hit from behind when you stop with the front bumper of your car before the stop line. Anyway, all of a sudden the car starts to shake, not the normal vibration you are used to, and I'm talking major shaking. After the car has come to a full and complete stop, put the car into park, then press the gas lightly and release. If that doesn't clear it up, one of the most common problems is that one of your spark plug wires may have popped off a spark plug. Because you have asked or have been shown, you can find this problem, fix it, and be on your way.

If the car is an automatic, you might have over-filled the transmission or you could be low on transmission fluid. Anytime you feel that something doesn't feel right, check your gas gauge. You learn as you go; just keep in mind, the maintenance of the motor vehicle is directly your responsibility.

Winter is the time of year when batteries have to be replaced when you least expect it. You have to keep in contact with your car. It's an extension of you and it's only a machine. Take care of it and it will be reliable transportation. Check your car out good in the fall to eliminate winter headaches.

***

If you find you have to constantly put new parts into your car., it might be a good idea to check the book value before you over invest. It might be the right time to clean it up good and sell it. You can see it coming by the repair bills. Keep all repair receipts to show that the car has been maintained properly. If you put new wiper blades on, keep the receipt. It's very impressive. It shows that you know something about the car. Do not sell to family members unless they have an excellent understanding of the car's condition. This way if something were to happen, it won't come back to you in the form of a bad attitude.

People get crazy when it comes to cars. Outside the family, sell it for the best price you can get. When you are buying a used car, check to see if the brake, or the clutch and brake black rubber pedal covers are new.

If they are brand new, I recommend the car be taken to a dealer to be checked out. Make sure they check all of the wheel bearings.

Wheels make or break the looks of the car. The wheels catch your eye. I have cleaned up old rims with fine sandpaper then sprayed them silver and they just changed the car's impression completely.

***

There is no way you can just enter the flow of traffic without checking for a whole lot of things first. The entrance to a highway is designed so you can pick up speed and enter the flow of traffic safely. You have to know how much room you have to pick up speed in. You are to accelerate on the entrance ramp, then if it is safe to do so, you enter the first lane. If you cannot enter the first lane safely, you must be prepared to slow down again and stop with your right directional on, showing the flow of traffic that you have done the smart thing. The smart thing is to see the situation for it's real worth.

All of this starts way back at the beginning of the entrance ramp. When you first turn onto the entrance ramp, you must find the center of your lane and make the necessary adjustments. Then you must know what's happening on your immediate left and right. You have to check your inside mirror somewhere during this maneuver.

People will cross the street more at the corners than in the middle of the block. I recommend that you know exactly what is behind you and what the driver is doing, just in case you have to stop. If you, and you will one day, have your vocabulary increased by a person crossing the road in front of your car, it is in your best interest to keep your mouth shut.

We do not, in general, walk around yelling at the top of our lungs. When you are walking, the cars and trucks make the louder sounds. Now all of a sudden you hear someone yelling. You turn and see a pedestrian yelling at a teenage driver and the teenage yelling back. It doesn't matter who is right or wrong, it's the teenage that stands out.

You can't help but notice that the front of the car is a direct threat to a pedestrian. With what you have heard and by what you see, and the reputation teenagers have when it comes to driving, the first thought that comes to mind will be that the teenager is at fault.

Maybe no one saw the pedestrian cross when the walk light changed or maybe this is a person who likes to cause trouble. It could also be that the person crossing ran out quickly and it was a display of excellent vehicle control that saved the pedestrian from his/her own stupidity. The only thing that anyone will see is the teenager. Guilty until proven innocent. So keep your cool and be polite and make your best impression.

After finding out how long the entrance ramp is, you have to check out the flow of traffic to see if you can enter safely. Cars travel in groups or packs. There will be 5-8 or maybe ten cars in a group or pack. A lot depends on the time of day. Then there will be a space with a few stragglers. There will then be another group of cars. The idea is not to race out in front of everybody. Its more like coming up behind them.

You must pace the flow of traffic so that you can enter the highway safely when the space between groups, or packs, of cars allows. The directional must be put on as soon as possible.

You must use the directional to show intent. Showing intent gives the drivers around you more time to re-check their surroundings.

When the entrance ramp meets the highway, you should be able to see the traffic both directly behind you and on the highway you are entering by using your inside mirror. Then you must check your blind spot to be sure that you didn't miss anything. As you come down the ramp, do not try to pick up a lot of speed right away. You may have to stop. Try to pick up only enough speed to enter the flow of traffic safely. Always remember you may have to slow down and wait for a better traffic situation to materialize. Keep your directional on until you have gotten into the center of the lane and you feel more comfortable with your newly found surroundings. Adjust your speed to match your pace, and down the road you go. If there is a car in front of you on the entrance ramp, you must always let it enter the highway first. Then you have the driver behind you who doesn't want to go all the way to the end of the line before getting into the first lane. They speed up and go around you cutting you off and forcing you to pull back to the right to avoid a crash. Expect it, one day it will happen.

***

Intersections. In this situation, there's a traffic light and at the light there is a north-bound enterance. The traffic going straight across the intersection is given the right of way. If you are trying to make a left turn at this particular intersection, you usually have to wait a long time. The last time we drove through this intersection, there was a car waiting to make a left turn and my alert student wound up stopping behind it because he didn't see the situation until he was in it.

When it did dawn on him that his path was blocked, he started to check his surroundings to find out that the flow of traffic had come up from behind him and boxed him in. I told the student to switch lanes, but the student chose not to. Now today, he makes the turn and there is nothing waiting at the light, so instead of staying in the lane that is going straight through, he changes into the lane that ends past the light.

Now I can understand this misunderstanding. So here we are with a stone wall representing the end of our lane. We had three cars behind us when we came off the exit and they went into the second lane heading straight across the intersection. They were joined by three more cars that had come up from behind. I had myself a tightly packed group of cars passing on my left and the wall. Just before the wall, there is a right turn into a residential area. I know the area well; if you have driven an intersection from all angles, and memorize stationary objects as you drive along, you can use the objects for reference. In this situation, the houses were spaced apart enough to allow the driver to see if there was an approaching vehicle on the road entering ours from the right.

And there was, and it was in the middle of the road being driven by an older man trying to light his cigar and fix his jacket at the same time. The student was totally oblivious to any of this. His eyes were straight forward. Now the student decides to change lanes, which consists of turning the wheel in a different direction. I took control of the vehicle, slowing it down before the corner. The student couldn't understand what was wrong. Then he says, blind spot, and checks his left blind spot to find bumper to bumper traffic passing him. I brought his attention to the back of the stop sign at the end of the road to our right. His reply was that the stop sign wasn't for him. I asked him "If you think the stop sign isn't for you, what makes you think the other driver thinks it's for him?"

And with that, the car entering from the right ran the stop sign. These are the types of situations we talk about all the time. The more objects you can identify, the safer you will be.

This could have gone another way. My student driver could have waited until the last minute, then seeing the car approaching from the right assuming it would stop, try to change into the second lane only to be forced back to the first lane by the flow of traffic. At this point, I could see the student looking at the cars on the left and getting hit by the car that blew the stop sign on the right. Intersections are killers.

This force could push our car into the second lane, then it could get worse. A car may try to avoid hitting us, hitting another car head on instead. The outcome of this whole situation was that we had to make a right turn. The car to our right ran the stop sign and slid to a stop, but not before forcing a car to go onto the double line to avoid contact. When we went around the block, the driver of the car that got cut off was stopped at the light and out of his car banging on the roof of the other driver's car. It seems there was a baby on board.

Remember…you don't know who is driving the other car. So try to be as inconspicuous as possible. Always be prepared to stop. Be prepared to change your direction or sound your horn at any time.

You will experience different intersection situations. During construction, the safe way may not always be clear. So, stay to the right as much as possible and always be polite.

***

In this class, we were approaching an intersection that was totally ripped up. They were at the point of construction where all they had to do was to put in loops and pave the road. The new curbs were in place and the sidewalk area was well defined. It was a long overdue improvement. All obstacles had been removed. Trees had been replaced with small evergreens and bushes. The usable road was well defined by construction barricades. There were larger orange and white four-foot tall items connected with orange mesh fencing. The path to follow was clear. The student driver had already proven to me that he is at this point a classic type A personality, so I'm expecting the worst and worse it got. He didn't consider the construction at all and proceeded to drive into the middle of what he considered to be his lane. When we got to the corner, we were in the center of the road.

Remember…only half of what you see is yours. The other half of the road is for the opposite flow of traffic.

I corrected the lane positioning and asked the driver what he thought he was doing. The driver turns to me and says, "Don't worry, they have enough room." Take it from a parent, when a teenager says, "Don't worry", the first thing you do is worry. We went around the block and parked on a side road overlooking the intersection in question. We watched the traffic to see how many other drivers would make the same mistake. As I was explaining what to look for in the future, a car stopped right where my student had. From our vantage point, we could see a car coming the other way. How they missed each other is a mystery to me.

When examples like this happen, I point to the clock and say whatever time it is and then I will say something like "Right on time," or "Thanks, talk to you later." During the first few weeks, I have students that think I set these situations up. There is really no need for that. As time goes on, students start to realize that these situations are all around them all of the time. If you think for them, you will see them.

***

The students are settling down now and are starting to talk. One student's reaction time is very slow, but the interest is there and so far I can see some improvement.

We were approaching an intersection with one car up ahead of us almost at the traffic light. We are back a good distance with a station wagon coming up fast behind us. I brought this to the driver's attention and we started to examine the situation. Judging the speed and lane position of the wagon, we determined it was going to pass, with no directional, over a double yellow line, approaching the stale green light. I told my student to check the center of the lane and to listen over his left shoulder for the sound of the passing station wagon.

Remember...when you first hear the sound of the car passing, you check your lane positioning and make any corrections needed, before the car passing enters your peripheral vision.

You hear it, and then you see it without turning to check your blind spot. If you bring your concentration close to you at the right time, your eyes relax and your peripheral vision opens. Your main point of concentration is always the same, and it's simple to understand. Driving is not a joke; it's your safety and the safety of the passengers that must always be in the front of your mind.

When the car passing reaches your driver's door, it enters your peripheral vision. This is the front end of the car passing you that were talking about. Hold your speed. The other driver is judging their actions based on your positioning. You have time to recheck your mirror and make any last minor wheel or lane adjustments as the car passing comes up alongside of you.

The critical point of passing is when the back bumper of the car passing reaches your driver's door, until the back end of the passing car has cleared the front end of your car by at least four feet. After the back end of the car passing passes your front tire, it is advisable to ease off the gas just a little bit and allow your car to slow down a little.

The idea of easing off the gas is to ensure a safe pass by allowing the passing car to clear the front end of your car sooner, but up to that point, you should hold your speed steady. You do not want to throw the other driver's judgement off by dropping back too soon. They might not expect it, so just think for yourself. Don't expect other cars to use their directional. It's nice when they do, and law requires it, but not everyone respects this common courtesy. When the car passing reaches the point where you can see into the back window of the car, you can see the actions of the driver. The situations are different but the outcome is almost always the same. What you are trying to see is when the other driver checks their mirror or blind spot to locate you so that they can change lanes again.

Remember…if a car passes you and you can see the back of the driver's head turn in the direction of their inside mirror or blind spot, take that as a directional. Sometimes you can see the driver's eyes in the mirror when they check it. This is easy to learn; take your time.

Some driver's only go by the rate of speed that they are passing at. To them, it took so long to pull up along side, so it should be a little longer time than that after you disappear out of sight into their right side blind spot for them to be clear to change lanes again.

This is not correct highway driving. This is a voluntary roll of loaded dice. It's a big mistake to expect that your blind spot will be clear without checking it. The highway is no place to drop your guard.

If a passing car starts to make its move back over too soon, you are ready to sound your horn. Not a happy pedestrian, toot, toot: you sound your horn with feeling and decrease your speed as necessary to avoid contact.

The station wagon went around us with no directional and we made sure there was enough space as it came back over. One of the comments that came from the back seat was, "What a jerk!" You could see that traffic had gathered on both sides of the road at the intersection up ahead, so we started to slow down. Sure enough, the light changed and the car that was now very close to the traffic light, hit the brakes to stop. The driver in the wagon hit the brakes and locked up all four wheels. The wagon turned sideways and slid a good 100 feet before coming to a very smoky stop about one foot or less from the stopped car.

As the wagon was skidding sideways, one back seat statement did sum it up in a nutshell, but I can't print it. This is the perfect example of an A type of personality. The driver took a big chance; it was a real stupid move. My students learned a good lesson in attitude, judgement, observation and control.

***

We always think to get the best gas mileage possible. The class is paying attention well and I feel this is one of my better classes. I'm trying to keep track of my gas mileage. When we get to the half way point, I am usually getting around 300 miles to the tank. Here, I am seeing the number 300 showing up. It means I have been successful in communicating with students. This class is off to the 8th floor-parking lot to learn some close quarter drills.

The first thing you do when entering a parking lot type building is to drop your speed down to 5 miles per hour and find the posted speed for inside the garage. See where you must stay. You could be entering a ramp that is going up, down or straight in. The turns are very tight going from one floor to the next, so you must visualize the true dimensions of your car or you could scrape up against something as you round the turn to the next level. If you enter the garage at say 25 miles per hour, then find the posted speed limit to be 15, you probably will not be able to reduce your speed fast enough. If you enter at the lower speed and then increase the speed, your chances of staying within the speed limit are greater.

Naturally I have voices asking, "What are they going to do, get me with the radar?" They don't need radar; all they have to do is see you playing the role of the fool. If you get what is referred to as a nice cop, you may only get one ticket. If you start running off at the mouth about how great a driver you are, the officer could ticket you into the greatest driver you ever were.

I recommend that the headlights be put on when you enter the garage. Always go for the best that you can make your presence known. This is where the checking out the front or back of the car is advised as you walk away from it. You always check the car before you walk away from it. Check for open windows, make sure that the keys are in your hand, and then lock the doors. As you walk away, put the keys in your pocket as you check to be sure that the lights are out. Then off you go with peace of mind. When you leave the garage, make sure that you remember to turn your lights off when you exit. I am talking in the daytime now.

Driving in one of these parking facilities is like driving through a pop up target range. One pop up situation is when you have a big car or van pulled in and a space on the other side. You can put a small car next to the big van and not be able to see it until it backs out. If there looks to you like there could be something there, there is something there. Until you can see that the area is clear, you must be prepared to stop and sound your horn to emphasize your presence.

Chapter 3

STUDENT COMMENTS

I have learned many things and also improved my weaker skills while driving during Driver's Ed. For most, I have come to feel much more comfortable driving major roadways like parkways. I could not have had so much experience on this type of roadway, but practicing while with a teacher has made me feel more comfortable merging, changing lanes, looking for signs and dealing with high speed and busy traffic. I also feel like my senses during driving have improved. I am much more aware of things that go on and things that could go on. I feel ready for many situations. Finally, I feel more practiced in driving and feel that having more experience has made me more capable on the road.

***

What I learned.
  Hand over hand recover:
  Before D.E., I just spun the wheel through my hands.
  Inside mirror:
  I used to use it just to fix my hair, now I look at a lot.
  Side Mirrors:
  I now know that they aren't necessary. I used to use them to change lanes and stuff.

***

I think Driver's Ed. made me more aware of the driving environment around me. At first I only used to concentrate on my ability and myself, but now I try to anticipate equally the other drivers as I do myself.

***

Wheel Control: my eyes are more open to cracks and defects in the road. I have more control in stopping fully and being more prepared and cautious for possible situations. I definitely feel more comfortable while driving.

***

I learned better wheel control and I glance in my rear view mirror more frequently. I also slow down sooner when I see a stop sign or red light ahead.

***

Driving on the highway and changing lanes and watching out for other Cars coming into the highway from an exit were the things that stood out during the lessons. I learned to maintain the first lane and slow down or accelerate whenever a car is entering a highway, allowing the other car to enter smoothly. I used to hesitate before I took lessons but I know now what to do and I feel great.

***

To date, Thursday is my best day. Everyone wants to learn and they all talk about driving. Even better than that, they're all the same size. This makes for a safer change when it comes to switching drivers.

***

We dropped off a student at school today. She got out the back door on the curbside. As soon as the door closed, the driver started to pull away. I stopped the car. The driver asked if it was because she started off too fast. I said the start was good, but you didn't check to make sure that the person had gotten away from the car first. This could be a problem. What if the passenger closes the door and his/her coat gets caught in the door? If this happens you could drag a person to their death. The driver's comment was along the lines of running the person over. This shows me that she and I are thinking in the same ballpark.

Remember…The driver is responsible for the safety of the passengers.

On a four-door car, the back doors are in the blind spot area. You must always turn and see with your own eyes that the person has moved away from the car before you go about trying to leave the curb and enter the flow of traffic.

***

We had to call off driving today because off the bad weather. It started to snow and it looks like we might wind up with an inch or so accumulation. It's cold out, but the humidity is relatively low. The snowflakes are small, but they have a tendency to melt very slowly, thus leaving an accumulation on the road. This is where your common sense must come into play. If you have a thin layer of snow on the road, it lays on top of the oil. To you, it looks like no threat, until you apply the brake. This is another form of black ice. It's not ice in the form of frozen yet, but the outcome of this combination of moisture and oil is the same. You are going to slide if you don't drop your speed down. Take your time. If the snow melts when it hits the road, the temperature is warm. Slow down. Occasional gusts of cold wind can freeze some spots and leave others wet.

When people see the blue sky, they seem to stop thinking. They forget that it is still winter and start thinking summer. That's all well and good but if you start to think summer and start to drive like its summer, it won't work. You have to make sure that you don't drop your guard. You have to be aware of the danger in this situation. Keep your speed down. Keep your concentration closer to you. People see the blue skies and go bananas. Take your time; be prepared to react in a controlled manner at all times. This will give you time to think.

***

Stopping before the stop line takes planning. If you see a car approaching a stop sign on the road coming toward you or off to your left or right side, you must check your inside mirror. What if a car were to pull out in front of you without warning? Knowing what's behind you is a key factor.

Remember…a car has not come to a full stop until you see the car come to a full stop, and then there is no guarantee the car will remain stationary. You only need to drop your guard once.

As situations go, in this situation the wet road or ice and snow could prove to be more than the other driver is prepared to handle. If the car approaching the stop sign starts to skid, it will come right out in front of you. If the car slides into your right side, it could push you into the oncoming traffic.

You must practice stopping with a good distance from the stop line every time you stop. You must develop your conditioned reflexes and one of the most important reflexes is to be able to sense danger. When the wrong things start to happen, it could be too fast for you to react to.

I practice last minute right turns with my students to keep them on their toes. Stay away from emergency left turns. Trying to cross over the oncoming flow of traffic at the last second could cost you your life. Spooky stuff.

Remember…you are not a bad driver; you are a new driver and you have to except the fact that you are still learning.

***

Defensive driving consists of a lot of correct positioning for best results. Now that's not supposed to be some kind of super intelligent statement; it's a way of opening your mind to the subject called driving. React to your first thought: most of the time you will be correct. If you're not correct, you still have time to correct it because you were taking your time.

Reacting to your first thought can also get you into deep trouble. You must memorize the sequence of actions to be taken before altering the speed or direction of the vehicle. You must be sure there is a space in the area you plan to occupy and you must understand that if someone else sees the possibilities, they will challenge you for the space.

***

The temperature has dropped a bit, and icy conditions have been reported in the general area. The speed has been lowered on all of the bridges because of the icing. Reports have come in about multi-car accidents on two of the local parkways. I am sitting here listening to one of the sounds of winter; it's my neighbor, stuck in the snow with his all-season radials.

He's really getting charged up now. At first, he started with a rocking motion. You give just enough gas to get the car to move about an inch or so, then ease off the gas. By doing this, you are checking to see just how much traction you have. Then foot to the brake and shift into reverse and give just enough gas to move the car about an inch or so to start off with.

Remember…you must take your foot off the gas to allow the engine to come down to an idle before changing gears. You do not, and I mean do not, shift directly from reverse to drive and vice versa until you have eased your foot off the gas pedal and let the motor quiet down to an idle.

Remember…your foot must be on the brake when you change gears. Don't run off with this yet. We are talking about rocking the car back and forth when you are stuck in the snow and we are talking about an automatic transmission. That is the one with two pedals: one is the gas and the other is the brake. The standard shift has a third pedal to the left of the brake. This is the clutch.

Now my neighbor is starting to lose his patience and I can hear the tires of his car spinning for longer periods of time. You have to clear a path to the best of your ability before trying to get the car out of the snow. My neighbor has all-season steel belted radial tires and swears by them. Now he is outside swearing at them.

If you buy a steel belted radial tire, you get a steel belted tire. If it's in the spring, summer, fall, or winter, it's still a radial tire. The effectiveness is in the tread.

I'm back; my neighbor has everybody looking out their windows. He is now smoking up all his seasons. It looks like The London Fog floating across my front yard. The damage he is doing by shifting back and forth from reverse to drive and back to reverse with the gas pedal almost to the floor may not show up right away. But it will, and when it does show up, it will be in the form of a very expensive transmission replacement.

***

Today was the first Saturday, that my Saturday class drove. All of the students seem to show good interest. This may very well rival my Thursday class. We still have to see as we go. Wheel control problems are to be expected. Use of directional leaves a lot to be desired, but their spirits are high. Most have no idea of the blind spot, so we will have to work with that. Setting the inside mirror seems to be falling into place. I have to work with that. I have to work a bit faster because of the snow days and vacation time. One student had never been behind the wheel before. Needless to say, it was a very eye opening experience to the other students and a good challenge for me, but I see good potential.

***

Blind spots seem to be the order of the day. Attitudes are good, so it turns into a 'time will tell' situation. One student seems to stand out today as improving. But, I have learned from past experiences that a student can drive good one week and the next week do something stupid. This is the part of my job that keeps me on my toes. I have to expect anything at anytime, and anything happens very often.

Remember…you do not, as of yet, have enough experience to guarantee that your conditioned reflexes will react correctly. You must pay attention to what you are doing all of the time. Good reaction time is a must. You cannot lose track of your surroundings.

The more situations you experience the sharper you get. With me, things happen so often that there is almost no break. You, on the other hand, have not experienced enough of the reality of driving yet. No problem: you learn as you go and if you want to, you'll do just fine.

The blind spots on your car are the areas that you cannot see when you check your inside mirror. The blind spots cannot be checked by peeking out of the corner of your eye. My students seem to be scared to take your eyes off the road to check their blind spots. You understand what is behind you by checking the inside mirror, and then you bring your eyes to the front. Don't think too far ahead. Think about identifying the objects close to you first while you think about what you saw in the mirror. Then you repeat checking the mirror until you feel comfortable.

You must establish your immediate surroundings first, and then you can check your blind spots with relative ease. Just how far should I be thinking to see? It's not how far; it's how much. By using reference points, you'll keep concentration close to you and identify objects at the same time. You are keeping your concentration close to you and identifying the mirror at the same time. Mirror road, mirror road.

The center of your mirror is to be your main point of concentration when the inside mirror is checked. When you bring your eyes back to the front, you are thinking about what you have seen in the mirror. Object, yes or no.

Not the name of the car or truck, not the color of the object. You must identify the presence of the object first. Then through the process of memorization, you can more clearly identify the objects. Stationary objects make excellent points of reference. If you relax, your peripheral vision will open and your concentration stays closer to you.

Let's put you in your kitchen, sitting down, looking forward, what's behind you? Now if you turn your body all the way around, you are looking at what is behind and you know what's behind you because you were just looking in that direction. Well, you just can't keep turning your body around when you drive; it just won't work. This is where the inside mirror comes into play. By checking the inside mirror, you can keep track of what's going on behind you. You can see if you are going to get hit when you're stopping. You can determine if you are going to get hit by a car that's trying to pass. It allows you time to judge the speed and distance of the car that's about to pass.

There are exercises designed to help you open your mind to your new surroundings. They will help you set the inside mirror correctly. They will help to keep your awareness even more consistent.

***

Today, we went over the dimensions of the car, and then we went to the parking garage. The eight-floor garage is great. Cars are moving all the time; people could walk right out in front of you. Baby carriages come around the corner before the person pushing it can see if it's clear. People open doors without looking. Cars back out without looking. Children could run out from between parked cars. Pop up targets, but in this case, they're real. The only thing is you're not supposed to hit anything. I thought it would be interesting and interesting it was. Tunnel vision was the biggest problem.

One student saw a car starting up. I told her to watch out for back up lights and ease off the gas. Faster than you can start to ease your foot off the gas, you can check your inside mirror and be prepared to stop if necessary. Thinking for reference points when you check your mirror shortens your reaction time and lengthens your stopping distance.

As we continued to drive forward, the back up lights came on and the car started to back out. The student did nothing; she just watched the car as it started to back out towards us. I had to apply the brake and sound the horn. I asked the student why she didn't react at all considering that I had just told her what to expect. She told me that she thought the other car was going to stop. That is a wrong answer. You have to check to see where the other driver is looking to determine if they see you or not. You could see very clearly that the driver of the other car was looking in the other direction.

The idea of a parking garage is to make the best use of the space available. You drive in and find a place to park, then walk to the elevator or take the stairs. You must be very careful walking around. Don't drop your guard when you get out of the car. That is a big mistake.

We pulled into a parking space to switch drivers. One student in the back seat checked over his shoulder to make sure it was safe to exit the car, then started to open the door. I told him to get back into the car and close the door. The driver was also trying to get out. I told her to get back into the car and close the door. Neither student saw what was wrong; they both asked what they had done wrong. The problem was that the driver had not put the car into park yet. The driver had put the car in reverse and the motor was still running. I had my foot on my brake, as I always do, keeping the car stationary.

When the students saw what was wrong, they started to argue about who was right and who was wrong. It turns out that both of them were wrong. It is the driver's responsibility to be positive that the car is secure before allowing passengers to exit the car. In the same respect, as the passenger, you must be positive that it is safe before you exit the car.

The driver is responsible for the safety of the passengers and the passengers must respect the position of the driver. The driver is calling the shots. It's not safe to exit a vehicle until the driver says it's safe to do so. I wouldn't like the car to start to move with me only halfway out.

**

In class today, we had a new driver behind the wheel and we were getting ready to go. The driver adjusts the seat and then puts his seatbelt on, but he does not pull it tight. You can think what you want, but if you only put the belt on and do not adjust it correctly, you are going to take a severe physical beating inside of your own car. The seatbelts must be on right. Pulling the belt tight promotes better posture. The better your posture is, the greater your ability to see your surroundings. The more conscious you are of your surroundings, the more confident you become with your actions.

It's a positive domino effect: observation, judgement, and control.

After a lengthy explanation, the driver was belted in correctly and all the back seat questions had been answered, we went back to leaving the parking space. The driver put his foot on the brake and applied pressure to keep the car stationary. The ignition switch was turned on. If the key does not fit, you may be holding it upside down. Remove the key and turn it over, then try again. If it still does not work, you must make sure it's the right key. It's easy to make this mistake. Just remove the key and check it out.

Remember…do not force the key. If you break it off, you'll have a bigger problem. Don't be afraid to seek assistance. And in the same respect, you must be prepared to lock your doors and sound the horn if approached by a menacing force. Learn how to sound "SOS."

So, now the key has been turned into the spring-loaded area and the motor springs to life. The driver has checked the blind spots and has made all the proper mirror adjustments. The driver turns and asks if he can go, and I say yes. My students are required to clear it with me before the car is taken out of park. This driver has a license. We are backing out to the left, so the driver has to turn his wheel to the left.

Remember…if you want the back end of the car to go left, you turn the wheel to the left. If you want your back end to go to the right, then turn your wheel to the right. Always keep track of the front end of your car when you back up. You don't want to hit anything with the front of your car.

Now this student puts a left directional on and then takes the gear selector out of park. As soon as the hand went to the directional, my guard went up. First off, the gear selection is done first. Then the directional goes on. What I have here now is his second mistake. In the sequence that I am observing, the next move will be to put the car into drive instead of reverse. And, sure enough, he looks straight at the gear selector and puts it into drive. Then he turns and looks out the back window and brings his foot to the gas. I had my foot down on the brake hard, so he wasn't going anywhere. When he touched the gas, and the car tried to go in the other direction, he almost shed his skin; he should have double-checked the gear selection he had made.

Now the first reaction in a situation like this is to get your foot back to the brake and regain control. This is a conditioned reflex and must be patiently practiced. This driver couldn't figure out what had happened. I had to tell him to take his foot off the gas, and put his foot on the brake and the car into park. Now it's time for a little chat. "Just what do you think you're doing, if you don't mind me asking?" The students in the back seat started to laugh while mister license man turned beet red. He tried to do a lot of fast talking, but the more he tried to cover up his mistake, the more the permit people in the back seat ranked on him. This form of group interaction is good, but must be kept in check.

His first big mistake was putting on the directional first. Being a new driver, he wanted to impress me with his ability and driving accuracy by using his left directional when he backed up.

What happened was this, he heard the sound of the directional blinking and because you must always use a directional when you make a turn, and most of the time you drive forward, he put the car into drive without thinking. We talked the situation through until all angles were covered. This was a good lesson. Again, it comes down to observation, judgement and control.

All of the students that drove through the parking garage today had no idea of the concept of thinking about what is close to you first and then with a sweeping motion, scanning the area around you. They all had the tendency of keeping their eyes straight forward. I told a student to find a parking space and to pull in. The student drove past a lot of parking spaces, but didn't pull in. I asked why we were taking the scenic tour of the garage and pointed out to the driver that we only had half a tank of gas. I asked if it would be enough. The student's reply was that the other spaces were too small. Not so.

I have seen situations where areas have been marked off for just compact cars, but this was not the problem. All of the spaces were the same size. The driver just could not judge the dimensions of the car. When you get into a different car, you have to check it out. No matter how many years driving experience you have, when you get into a different car you must find the areas that are hardest to judge first. Different cars have different size blind spots.

One student was complaining about not being able to see. A helpful voice from the back seat suggested that the driver use a phone book. The driver started to laugh then asked me if I had a phone book. I always carry a phone book, so I got it out of the trunk for her. She was amazed at how much more she could see. She kept saying, "Look what I can see," and, "This is great!" I will not be surprised if she brings a pillow to class next week. You might be surprised how much a cushion could do for you.

First off, cars are made with the average person's height in mind. You might not reach your full height until you are 19 or 20 years of age or older. You know how confusing it can be when you can't see something. I keep the phone book to use as an example; sitting on a phone book for long periods of time could be very uncomfortable. Try a phone book first and see the difference and then buy the right size cushion for you.

Well, let's go, you have something to do. Check and see if maybe you could benefit from a cushion of some sort.

***

The weather is a big part of driving, and the weather today was not good. They are calling it a storm; I think it's great. The waves are coming over the ten-foot sea walls with ease. The winds range from an almost constant 20-MPH to 40–60 mile per hour gusts. If this rain were snow, it could be up to the second floor of houses. The weight of the snow would have destroyed many houses, but it's not snow.

When the rain comes down in sheets driven by the wind, it creates a major visibility problem. You will find that even though you have your wind shield wipers on high speed, they will not be able to move the water off your windshield fast enough for you to see where you are going. You may have to open your window and peek to see if you are safe at the moment. If you just stick your head out into the rain, it will go into your eyes causing a bigger problem. If the wipers throw off a blade, you get one out of your trunk, put it on, and go about your business.

If you lose your wiper blade, you might have to lean over to see out the passenger side of the windshield as you pull over to stop. As soon as you are safe, turn the wipers off to prevent scratching the windshield.

Remember…your safety always comes first. You are not thinking to damage the car in any way, shape or form, but sometimes things happen. If you lose a wiper blade and turn them off so that you won't scratch the windshield, you might be defeating your purpose by further limiting your ability to see. Replacing the windshield is not a problem. You will have to replace many things as you drive day to day for years.

***

We were going over opening your car door today. Whenever you pull over, you must be really careful getting out of your car. Just because the car has come to a stop doesn't mean you are safe in any shape or form. You must make sure that the car is put into park with the parking brake on before you turn the car off. You must identify the actions of all your passengers. You must keep your foot on the brake until you have checked the mirror and over your left shoulder. Four way emergency flashers should be used to make your presence known. I have to back up a bit here. You have to make sure that when you open your door that it doesn't go over the right side lane marker into the first lane. If a car hits the door, it could slam it shut on you, ruining your day or terminating your existence.

Remember…here comes the common sense stuff again. If it doesn't seem safe to you, don't do it. Always stay where you can see and where you can be seen.

Back to the weather…The wind just took my neighbors' garbage can cover away. It just went up and out of sight. To give you a better idea how strong the wind is, as the lid was going up in the air, it hit some phone wires, then flew up to the top of the telephone pole and hit the electrical wires. It flipped over a few times then went straight up out of sight. A few of the roofing tiles on my neighbor's house are flapping in the breeze. They just banned all tractor-trailers, motorcycles, and car-pulled trailers from all of the major bridges in the area. That should give you a good idea of the force involved. Thousands of people are killed each year because they were driving small cars.

In this type of weather, you must be very sharp in knowing your surroundings, especially in highway situations. You could get blown off the road if you are not paying attention. If you see that you are approaching an area where there are open fields on both sides, the chances of cross winds are excellent. How strong it is going to be can be difficult to determine. In dry weather, one way is if you see leaves blowing across the road. If the leaves are having a good old time blowing across the road like a flock of spooked birds, you could experience some steering discomfort when you reach that area. If you are planning to change lanes, I highly recommend you wait until after you pass through this cross wind weather situation. Then, when it is safe to do so, change lanes.

***

We were driving down the road today, and I told the driver to hold the wheel tighter. This is a good student, so without question, she held the wheel tighter and in the next instant we were hit by a strong gust of wind. I told the student to bring her concentration closer to the front of the car and concentrate on the center of the lane and she did very well.

This observation drew a lot of questions from the students. How did I know there was a gust of wind? We got off the parkway and went back. We stopped on the side of the road just before the spot where we had felt the gust of wind. I pointed to the tall patches of grass that were in the field and told the students to watch and see if the wind blows them over and holds them down for a second or so. It happened a few times and one gust of wind even picked up some dirt from along side the road. It was very impressive; I could not have planned it any better myself.

Remember…keep your concentration close to you and think about your surroundings as you travel. You have to look for everything all the time. To do that, you have to relax and stop trying to beat the clock.

***

Today the weather conditions kept us off the road, but it gives us time to talk about the weather. Today's weather can do anything it wants. They called for rain, then it is supposed to turn to snow. The problem is that the temperature is dropping faster than expected. This could change the expected rain to snow instead. Right now, everything is starting to be covered by a thin layer of ice. Its called freezing rain. The drop in temperature below freezing will turn the water on the road to ice. The snow will then cover the ice. Even the most experienced drivers are caught off guard by the elements. It looks like snow until you try to stop.

The worse the weather conditions are, the slower you drive. Think about the speed you are traveling and the distance you must keep from other cars. If something happens, you must have time to act correctly.

Remember…you must have enough distance to come to a sliding or skidding stop without hitting whatever is in front of you. The worse the conditions, the more stopping distance you need. It's that simple.

If the temperature goes up and down and it starts to snow, you can wind up with slush. It splatters all over the place. If a car passes, it could spray slush on your windshield. It will spook you, but you can't allow it to cause you to lose control. Check your mirror and ease off the gas. Think stability. If it is really cold out, your windshield washer fluid could freeze on your windshield when you spray it. Please be aware of that. You can buy windshield washer fluid that is formulated for cold weather from your auto parts store.

Make sure you know the positioning of the cars around you and expect to see mistakes. If you are in a slush situation and approaching a bridge, you must bring your concentration closer to you and ease off the gas. Check your mirror and find the center of your lane before you start to cross the bridge. Bridges freeze first, due to the wind chill factor. Another problem is falling ice. Ice covers the cables on the bridge and as the temperature goes up, the ice starts to fall off. If there is a lot of ice falling, they may close the bridge completely. This can cause delays. Keep an eye on the gas gauge. This is no time to run out of gas. Don't tell yourself that you will get gas in the morning. Get gas before you park your car and check all fluids as needed.

Remember…you must clean all ice and snow away from the windshield wiper blades before you turn the wipers on. If the wipers are frozen to the windshield and you turn them on, you could burn out the electric wiper motor. Clean away all ice and make sure the defroster is putting out heat before you use the windshield washers. Washer fluid is not used to melt ice; it is used to clean the windshield. De-Icer is for ice. You must remove the snow from around the exhaust pipe before you start the car. If you get into the car and start it without clearing the snow away from the exhaust, the exhaust fumes could find their way into the car. If this happens, it could kill you. Get into the habit of checking things right the first time.

Remember…Personal safety comes first.

Driving in a group situation brings out personalities faster. The worst personality to have behind the wheel in a bad weather situation is the "Devil May Care Attitude". This is no time to play.

You should notice if the branches on the trees are covered with ice. If the wind blows the ice off, and it comes down on your car, it will spook you. If you don't expect it, it will scare the heck out of you. There's a lot to think about, if you think about it. If anyone tells you that driving is boring, don't ride with them.

The build up of ice on branches in the trees will cause dead branches to fall off. You always expect falling branches. They can fall on top of your car as you are driving along, at any time. When you hear the weather report predicting icy conditions, try your best to stay on the main roads and stay away from trees as much as possible.

Remember…The stronger the winds are, the greater the chances of falling branches or trees. Keep your concentration close to you and slow down.

The rewards of being an instructor are few, but it all seems worth it when you see a student make a turn and recover using perfect hand over hand steering. The student sat up straight after the turn and told me that he had been practicing. You could see satisfaction and self-confidence beaming from his face. I was very impressed; the students in the back seat started to applaud his masterful display of wheel control. One back seat student said that she had been practicing, but that she can't turn the wheel back fast enough. I kept this statement in mind, and when we switched drivers, I asked the driver to make some turns so that I could help her correct her difficulty. Her problem was simple and easy to correct.

She was trying to drive like everyone else and was way off her pace. So staying on the side roads, I slowed the speed of the car down until she was able to complete a turn using hand over hand steering.

What I did was help her to find her pace. At 5 miles per hour, she had excellent control. Then we increased the speed to 10 miles per hour and she was all over the road.

We slowed the speed down again and she fell right back into place. The student in the back seat who had displayed such great improvement moments before praised the driver's progress with the comment, "He's right," meaning me, "listen to him, he knows, once you find your pace it's real easy. Take your time and practice like I did, you'll get better."

This is one of my better classes. All of the students in this class are trying to learn. When a student comes to class with an open mind, they will learn. It's the know-it-all attitudes that cause the problems. You can't know it all; it just doesn't work that way.

Remember…everyone's pace is different so you have to take your time.

***

Some students have problems understanding that the directional is to be used to indicate any change of direction, when-ever you change direction. I have found that some students think that the drivers around them know what they are going to do, so they just drive into situations and don't think about the consequences. One student made a wide right turn over the double yellow line and almost hit a car head on. I had to take control of the car to avoid collision. I asked the student just what the heck he thought he was doing and he just started to laugh. Driver's Education is not playtime. An instructor should be able to drop a student if they intentionally drive in an unsafe manner. The other students in the car told me that they didn't want to drive with him anymore, and I don't blame them. Considering the speed and position of the cars involved, if we had hit head on, someone could have been hurt.

Sometimes if a person does something stupid, they laugh to cover it up because they know they're wrong and have no sound explanation for their actions.

Remember…When you turn the key to the car, you accept the responsibilities of an adult.

***

It's another day, and the sky is blue, with light winds. These are the days to be very careful of. People see the nice weather and drop their guards. Windows are open and radios are on, and turned up loud. If you want to sing along when you're not moving, that's ok.

Remember…music effects both sides of the brain. If you see a car coming down the road with the occupants singing and moving to the music, this is to be considered a direct threat to the safety of the flow of traffic, and the situation is to be considered a direct threat to you. You must learn to see these situations and appreciate them for their true worth.

As we are driving along we are talking about our surroundings. Off to the right we notice a very obvious problem. It's a red car with dark tinted windows and the windows are closed. The car is coming down an entrance ramp towards a yield sign. Everyone in the car agreed that the car was going to run the yield sign and pull out in front of us. It was great. All the students started to tell the driver what was around him as he checked the mirror and eased off the gas to establish better distance. Sure enough, the car pulled right out into the flow of traffic. Being back far enough gave us the opportunity to see our prediction come true. All of the students were overjoyed with the fact that they predicted that it would happen. And it did. This is self-confidence. It is the ability to sense danger and the sense to stay away from it. I felt that extra credit was in order.

***

I like observations; too much explanation can be confusing. If you take your time and watch what you're doing, things will fall into place. Personalities and driving go hand in hand. Most of my students have settled down; now we can get into serious driving.

Remember…Gauges are the best. With gauges, your chances of detecting a problem are greater. The faster you can detect a problem, the less chance of damage to the car. It makes sense to me.

You must learn to know where your feet are by feeling contact with the bottom of your foot, through your shoe. Please do not try to drive a car without supervision. I know you think you're good and all that, but you owe it to yourself to have as much control as possible. This book is designed as an exchange of information that should be considered by the new driver as food for thought. These are my observations and opinions of different situations and their possible solutions, that's all.

Remember…you must find your pace first. You must stay calm. Patience, patience, patience, along with repetition, repetition, repetition will lead you to conditioned reflexes.

Well, we are moving right along here and I would like to say hello to all of you who are still awake. I hope you are starting to find yourself a little more comfortable when it comes to talking about driving. The goal is to feel more comfortable behind the wheel.

When you check your mirror, you are thinking to see what's directly behind you. I mean you are thinking to see no further than a two-foot distance from the back of the car. If you think deep into the mirror, you will see what's far back and miss any activity closer to the back of the car. If you think closer to you, you can't help but see what's in the background.

Remember…always think about what is closest to you first, then you can start to scan out further for more information.

Rule # 1: Everything moving is a threat to me and because I am in motion, I am a threat to myself.

Rule # 2: Always remember rule # 1.

Don't be in a rush: take your time. You have to get into the habit of checking at least twice before you consider making a move. You must be positive that you know where things are. Then you must keep tabs by checking now and again to make sure you see any changes in the flow of traffic or pedestrian activity. With your foot on the brake, put the car into gear. Shifters have safety devices to hold them in park and they work great, if used correctly. Check the owner's manual on the proper way to take the car out of park before you even start the car.

Floor shifters have something you press down, or pull up, or maybe you have to press a button on the side of the lever. It's much easier to read the owner's manual first. The last thing in the world that you need is a problem getting out of park. If you are concentrating too much, you could ease off the brake. If you have managed to pull it out of park it could start to roll. If it does pop out of park, you're staying still, with your foot on the brake. After the car is placed into gear, it's time to take the emergency brake off. In the time it takes to do all this, your surroundings keep changing.

Rule # 3: Just because it's not moving, doesn't mean it won't. I expect everything all of the time because it happens.

I check the inside mirror first to get a good idea of what's behind me. When I check my blind spots, I also check for eye contact. If you stare at a car, it is harder to judge the speed. If you check once and then again, you can compare the pictures in your mind, it's easier. You use your eyes differently when you drive. Your main point of concentration is your entire surroundings. When you check your blind spot for the second time, you must be thinking to see the difference between what you remembered and the new picture that you see. After practicing, you get good at judging the speed of the approaching car by how close it has gotten to you between glances. Check as many times as needed to insure safety.

This is where your pace comes in. Nothing is moving at the same speed. Everything is subject to acceleration or deceleration.

Remember…when you ease your foot off the brake, you must keep your foot over the brake until you are sure that the wheels are turned in the direction that you really want to go. If the car starts to head off in the wrong direction, you can press the brake again and stop safely.

Remember…the directional is always a must. You must always use your directional signal.

There is a lot to think about when it comes to driving. If you have to put the directional on, your hand goes to the directional and then it goes back to the 10 o'clock position. The left hand is to be where it belongs, no short cuts. If you don't have good steering, you're not driving, your only aiming.

I would like to take a moment to remind you that the observations and opinions you are reading are meant to be food for thought. You must ask as many questions as possible. Pick the best of your knowledge, then create your own driving habits. And always have an adult with you when you practice. Your insurance is high enough: don't drive unless it's legal.

***

We were on the highway today practicing lane changing. This is an art, not just a maneuver. You must have your full concentration on what you're doing. We were in the first lane. We had just passed an exit on the right and a distressed vehicle off to the left of the third lane.

With a good distance from the cars in front and a good distance from everything behind, I told the student to change to the second lane. She brought her concentration closer to her to ensure proper lane positioning. She checked her inside mirror, putting the left directional on at the same time. I was very impressed. You know what that means: that's right, it's time for something to go wrong. She checked her left side blind spot then thought about what she had seen. Then she made a big mistake. She didn't check her inside mirror again.

Objects in the mirror are closer than they appear but you sure can tell how fast they're going. When she checked to the left side blind spot for the second time, she wasn't sure if she had enough room to make the lane change.

When she checked the blind spot she should have been thinking to see the position of the truck clearly. Checking the inside mirror the second time, and thinking to locate the approaching pick up truck could have given her enough information right then and there. She should have seen the truck 3 times before checking the blind spot for the second time.

This is a licensed operator that is showing good signs of improvement. She had more than enough time to determine speed and distance.

Her problem was this: her concept of speed and distance has not been developed to it's fullest yet. A big factor here is your depth perception. The other major offender is tunnel vision. It comes down to practicing at low speeds during the time of the least amount of traffic and stay to the right. Not being able to understand the situation, she froze. These things happen to people: it's called dropping your guard.

Anyway, I stepped in. She did the right thing by not changing lanes. Judging by the information she had, she found herself in a state of confusion. What is the best thing to do in a state of confusion? You get out of it safely.

The reason we needed to change lanes was because a car was coming down the entrance ramp and entering the first lane. He didn't check for anything. He just pulled right into traffic doing a brisk 35-mph.

He shifted a gear and now with even more smoke coming from the back of the car, he drifted into the second lane and almost hit a passing car. Here is where it starts to get good. The car decided to slow down in the second lane and voice an opinion. From what we could see, the driver in the second lane was very strong in his beliefs and voiced them freely.

The car had pulled out in front of two cars in the first lane cutting them off. The first of the two was a big car. Now with the car in the second lane slowing down to argue, it took away an out, blocking the big car in the first lane from changing lanes.

And the brakes went on. It looked like a big hungry dog about to eat its lunch. The car behind the big car in the first lane was starting to leave tire marks on the road. I was able to avoid the situation by thinking to see it, then by reacting to it and taking the most obvious out. Close as it was, there was no contact. Everyone went his or her way. My students learned a good lesson in proper lane usage. I had seen the situation coming down. The best move that we could have made was to get into the second lane and give the driver behind us the option of passing us in the third lane. If the big car had chosen to make a dash to the third lane, the pick up truck would never have been able to stop in time. We had no problem. We had enough room. No matter what happened ahead, we had enough room to stop.

I feel that the student is now aware of the situation, and will act correctly again in the future.

If I hold up my hand, open palm, and ask you how many fingers I am holding up, the most common reply is 5 fingers. My answer would be four fingers and a thumb. You think you are correct in your assumption, based on the information that you believe to be true. Then you are introduced to an acceptable explanation that's different from yours, but with the same conclusion.

A good thing to remember is the fact that people react differently in different situations. I held my hand up and asked a student how many fingers I was holding up and she said she couldn't count that high. That was a wrong answer. I asked her a question and she was wrong. I sat back and waited, then I asked her again. This time the answer was a confident 5 fingers. Then I informed her that she was wrong twice. She didn't appreciate hearing it, but what if she were driving though an intersection and someone just stepped out? Could she react to the situation? Would the realization of fear cause a positive or negative response?

Remember…Most of the time that you're driving, you will be by yourself.

***

Today I put a football player onto the highway for some lane changing practice. If his performance behind the wheel is in any way at all close to his performance on the football field, I know what school to bet against this year. We meet at an open lot. He drives like he is some kind of super special person. Put him behind the wheel of a car on the highway and he folds up.

At the end of the lesson, he commented that driving was a lot more than he thought it was; anybody will tell you that, it's just that it sounds funny when you hear yourself admit to it for the first time. It takes a cool hand and a clear mind to stay in control. When you turn the key, you become a driver. Until you can see yourself as a driver, all you are doing is aiming the car.

***

Working with a large number of students allows me the good fortune of being able to observe a lot of students and their driving habits. Then we have the late bloomers. One of my students made a right turn today and recovered with a perfect hand over hand motion. His eyes got big and my guard went up. He looked at me with an ear to ear smile and in his excitement, put the gas pedal to the floor. I took control as the smile disappeared from his face.

It's a common mistake that a lot of drivers make. Hey, just because you have straightened out, doesn't mean it will go in that direction. We went up on the grass and back onto the road. It wasn't a big problem. The big problem was when I gave control of the car back to him; he put his foot down on the gas pedal instead of the brake. You could see by his actions that he knew his foot was on the wrong pedal, but he couldn't seem to move his foot over to the brake. Every time I told him to move his foot, he would press down on the gas. The students in the back started to laugh. I had to take control. We switched drivers.

This young man was laughing and joking about what had just happened, but I could see he was also concerned about his actions. This is where practice comes into the picture. You just have to know where your feet are and what they're doing. In the same respect, you can't drive around looking at your feet all the time either.

The next student to drive was very over confidant. He was stopping over stop lines. He kept his eyes straightforward and was not making any attempt to use his peripheral vision. He wasn't using the inside mirror and didn't seem to appreciate my correcting him. Bad habits are easy to get into, and difficult to break. The driver has a license and still brings his foot directly from the gas to the brake without any pause. This could be a show-off type thing, or maybe Mr. Know-It-All really doesn't know it all.

Off to the highway we go to practice some lane changing. This young man had a hard time just getting into the first lane. We switched drivers again. When I see that my students are confused or just spaced out, I tend to switch drivers a few more times than usual. It seems to bring them back down to earth and closer to the true reality of driving and the true reality of driving is safety.

Remember…you are not a bad driver: you are a new driver and it takes time to get it all together. Find your pace; stay on the small quiet roads until you feel confident to tackle the main roads and then work your way up to highway driving.

***

What about U Turns? A U-turn is always a dangerous maneuver. I probably have said it before, and if I have not, here it is. Stay away from

U-turns: too many things can go wrong. If you lose control and slide across the road and hit something, it is your fault. Nobody wants to hear you telling a story about how you thought you had enough room to make it. The chances of having an accident trying to make a U-turn are excellent.

If you slide into an oncoming car while you are pulling a U-turn, it is your fault. If a car comes out of a side road and you hit it trying to make a U-turn, it's your fault. If you hit a pedestrian while making an illegal turn, it is your fault. If you lose control of the car in the excitement of the moment and go up onto the sidewalk and kill somebody, it's your fault. Too many things can go wrong. Being a defensive driver, you understand that the idea is not to take chances.

If you approach an intersection and you see that you have a lane that is opening up on the left side, this is not a U-turn lane. This extra lane is for a left turn. Different states have different laws. In one state, you may not be able to make a U-turn where in another state you can. It doesn't take away from the fact that making a U-turn is not a safe thing to do.

Roads are getting more attention due to the increase in the volume of traffic, through the years engineers have started to place lanes that go off to the right then swing back to the left to meet the main road again. These are an excellent idea and are long overdue. This gives you, the driver, a safer way of reversing direction and decreases accident potential.

One of my students came back with, "My mother says it's ok as long as no one is there." To me that means there is not a soul in sight and there's no sign of vehicular activity at all. But if you have a pedestrian in the picture, how much distance from you is to be considered a threat. Should you make a U-turn? Now we start to get into exceptions to the rule. Once you have made an exception to the rule, you have dropped your guard.

Most of the time exceptions to the rules are just explanations for our actions that cover up a mistake that we are fully aware of, but don't wish to admit to. If you make one exception to the rule, you probably will make another somewhere down the line.

Then one day, you meet up with another driver who feels that their exception to the rule is more justified than yours. Yes, there are exceptions to the rules in certain situations. Circumstances will determine exceptions. If it's done to benefit you and you alone, in the moment that you determine it's best for you, then you have forgotten about everyone else around you. This would be your classic A type personality.

If you get pulled over and you tell the officer that you didn't know that you couldn't make a U-turn, well think about it: it's a statistically proven dangerous action. If you're not smart enough to see the danger in your actions, the police sure are and are always ready to voice the public's opinion by issuing a ticket for your actions.

This reminds me of a story that one of my students told us about driving home from their last vacation. The student said that he drove a good part of the way and was staying within the posted speed limit. His father kept telling him to speed up, but he stayed at the posted speed limit anyway. Now he told us that this went on for over an hour. It got to the point where my student decided that he didn't want to hear it anymore and located a safe place to switch drivers. And you know what happened, don't you?

As soon as his father pulled onto the highway and got up to the speed that he was telling my student to drive at, a Trooper came out of nowhere and gave his father a ticket. It was quiet the rest of the trip.

***

Today can be best described as, snow, snow, snow and more snow. What a beautiful winter's day! The clocks might as well have come to a stop. All plans are changed when the elements decide that we need a day off. Most people get crazy when it comes to snow. Even cleaning the sidewalk is an art in itself. It's well into the day now and we have more than a foot of snow.

What a beautiful day! It was an excellent day to get out and walk around. The gusts of wind went on all day. No trailers of any kind were allowed on the bridges. The radio had an advisory telling small cars crossing the bridges to keep their speed down because of dangerous cross winds. Well that's a nice thing to know; getting blown off a bridge is not exactly my idea of fun.

Anyway, I spent 2 ½ hours fighting to make some kind of dent in the snow on my walkway. Great work out! You let the tool do all of the work. The air was crisp, cool, and clear; what a beautiful day!

***

Here we are again: it's the next day. It was a fast hour clean up for me in the morning and my walks are clear. Even though it is cold out, the sun is shining on the clean walks and will start to dry them off. I had about four inches on my walks and my neighbors were shoveling 12 to 15 inches or more, not counting the snowdrifts. You have to take care of it when it's still coming down. It's much easier to do it that way. It's not like you don't have the time.

It was great. Once in a while, a car could be seen on the highway but there was really no traffic to speak of. In the afternoon, my neighbor was out with his electric snow blower; what a joke. You could hear the sound of the motor, it was screaming for snow until it was pushed into it. Then it gave out a sound similar to the last sound you hear a room fan make that tells you it's time to cut off the cord. He pulls it back and it runs faster again. He pushes it into the snow and it stops. This went on for hours and hours.

I was thinking about the snow when I parked my car. I parked it where the sun would be on the windshield for most of the day. I do this to help keep my wipers from freezing to the windshield. Most of the time, if you get the snow off early, the sun will dry the car.

Remember…you have to remove all of the ice and snow away from the windshield wiper blades before you start the car. If the wipers are frozen to the windshield and you turn them on, you could burn out the electric wiper motor. They must be clear of ice or snow.

De-Icer is good. Putting hot water on cold windshield glass will cause the windshield to crack. Some things are never done. Stay away from using hot water. No hot water on cold glass, the glass will break.

Always remember…never put hot water on cold glass.

When you clear the snow off of your car, you must never—and I mean never—use a snow shovel. What are you going to do is scratch the paint and we don't want to do that; use a brush, or a broom. Take your time. If you are working with a lot of snow, move some of the snow on the ground to make room, then clean the snow off the windows and clear it away from the car. When you push the snow off the hood and the trunk, don't try to push it all off in one shot.

***

Driving is done with ease. Your contact with the accelerator is your foot. Your foot can push a little or push a lot. There are many fuel adjustments that have to be made as you drive. You can feel a point of pressure with your foot and you may apply pressure with your foot to get the car moving. Then you ease off the pedal somewhat. You apply a comfortable amount of foot pressure to the gas pedal, enough to allow you to hold a comfortable speed for your particular driving situation, and down the road you go.

You have to practice working with the gas pedal. Practice easing off the gas pedal slightly, thinking to feel the car rolling on its own, then apply just a touch of very light foot pressure to the gas and then pause. It will take the motor a moment to react to the new amount of fuel. This is where you save gas but you must allow enough time for the car to pick up speed. This is not a problem; it just takes practice. If the foot pressure seems correct, keep a constant pressure and maintain your desired speed.

Because you are not familiar with the car, it will take some time to become familiar with the different reactions you will experience when different foot pressures are applied. After a while, you will become very much in control of your actions. You will practice to the point where you can relax your foot slightly and after that slight motion you will feel the car holding it's own. You will stay at the required speed and save fuel at the same time.

First off, you must be positive. You are not challenged to do the speed limit. Stay well below the limit and stay out of the main flow of traffic. You have to think to see signs. They don't just pick out signs and put them on the road where they think they might look good. The many different road signs that we have are intentionally placed to control the flow of traffic. If you disregard the signs, you are defeating the purpose. You will find situations where the road signs are missing. This is where common sense comes into the picture.

If you drive down a road every day and there is a stop sign nailed to a tree at the corner, you know to stop. If one day the wind blows the tree over and down on its side covering the stop sign, that does not mean that you no longer have to make a full stop. Any time you approach an intersection, you must be mentally prepared to stop, whether there is a sign there or not. The intersections are the biggest threat to your safety. Get into the habit of checking your inside mirror before you get too close to the intersection.

As you learn to judge your speed and distance better, you will find a happy medium. Working with the speed and distance factor for a while will give you better maneuvering ability. Say you see something up ahead, when you check your inside mirror and ease off the gas just a bit, you are allowing your mind time to better understand what's behind you and at the same time you open your ears more to better identify the sounds around you.

Remember…when you drive, the front end of your car raises up a bit. As you ease off the gas, the weight of the motor settles down onto the struts and increases stability and control. The car must use up this forward momentum. You got it going, now it takes time to slow it down. This is where the practice comes in. You see the situation up ahead, so you check to find if there is anything directly behind you, then as you ease off the gas, you let the car start to slow down by itself.

Remember…when you ease off the gas, the car will continue to roll. The motor has now gone to a lower revolution per minute than the transmission and this creates a drag. You can actually feel it slowing down. You can use this to your advantage. Your brakes will last longer if you use this method to prepare to stop.

Driving is a lot like flying, just that you never leave the ground, well, we're not supposed to. It's a way of getting from place to place in a safe manner, in a shorter amount of time than walking.

Sliding in a turn can be a problem, but every car rolls over differently. So we try to stay away from roll-overs. By intentionally keeping familiar distances from the cars around you, you can determine the best course of action. You have to stay calm enough to be able to make the best decision that you can; then you have to be yourself enough to take control and follow through with what you think is right.

There are many problems with turns, but I am yet to find one that can't be rounded safely using nothing more than common sense. Think about what you see and keep your mind moving with your eyes.

There is one standard move that can be applied to almost every driving situation. This is to ease off of your gas pedal slowly when you see the car up ahead enter the turn. If at the three-quarter point in the turn, the car up front of you taps the brake, you should ease off your gas pedal more. By the time you reach the point in the turn where the other car hit their brakes, you will have lost enough speed to round the turn without using your brakes. If you still need to slow down, because your car is slowing down anyway, you will need to use less brake. If at that point in turn you found, for some reason that you have to slow down more or stop, it's not a problem because you are prepared. This gas pedal adjustment allows you more time to check your inside mirror and make any minor adjustments to insure that you are in the center of your lane, as you think about what you saw in your mirror…very kicked back, take your time.

The flow of traffic will tell you a lot: you just have to take your time and allow yourself time to see it. Easing off the gas slowly will bring different reactions in different cars. You have to practice.

One day, for example, I went on the highway with an afternoon class to do some blind spot practicing. This is one of my better classes. The atmosphere in the car is excellent. They all like to drive and they all like each other.

We were in the first lane below the speed limit. Two cars that we had been discussing passed us on the left. One was in the second lane; the other was in the third. At one point we were equal, three abreast. This is in a wooded setting and the road is poured concrete, but it's old and a lot of stones in the concrete are exposed. The more of these stones that are exposed means that you will have to increase your stopping distance and adjust your reaction time by lowering your speed. The car in the second lane took off down the road like a bat out of hell. Up ahead of us, about four car lengths or so ahead of us, he decides to change into the first lane. This young man was rushing to his own funeral.

We had some distance to go before we entered a long, gentle right turn. Both of the cars had passed us and were well up ahead when my student identified a deer in motion alongside the road in the distance. This was an excellent call; my student even eased off of the gas before I told him to do so. It's nice to see students learn and this student got a round of applause from the back seat.

The two cars up ahead went into the turn with the car in the first lane in the lead. The car in the first lane was super driver, and he was about to meet super deer. At the halfway point in the turn, the deer started to run across the grass towards its young. The driver in the first lane hit his brakes. By the time he got to the three-quarter point in turn, he had locked his brakes up completely. He slid into the second lane leaving four dark skid marks, and a large amount of tire smoke. He slid across the second lane and hit the car in the third lane. They both went off the road into the grassy area, and slid to a safe stop. The drivers got out of their cars and walked over to each other. Judging by the hand motions it looked to me that the driver of the car that was pushed off the road was checking to be sure that the guy that hit him was all right. Then with a right cross, he put him flat on his back.

The contributing factors in this situation were: speed, judgement, observation and control. I'm not going to break it down in categories; I'm going to explain how I read the flow of traffic.

The car in the first lane behind us cut off the car in the second lane. The car in the second lane changed to the third and started to pick up speed. The driver changed out of the first lane without any warning. He just upped and changed lanes.

From what I saw, he was going by his outside mirror when he changed lanes. When we were three abreast, I was looking at the driver next to us to see what he looked like. The driver in the third lane was also looking at the driver in the second lane but he seemed more intent on conveying strong verbal statements of disapproval about the driver's inappropriate lane change. We eased off the gas to avoid danger.

Going by what I had already seen, and then not being in the center of the lane after passing us, showed us without question that the driver was a definite A type personality. The driver didn't check his inside mirror at all. This tells me that he was judging by his outside mirrors only. This is tunnel vision to the max. You can't forget your blind spots.

Remember…when a car has passed you, you can see into the back window of the car. You can locate the inside mirror in the passing car and determine if the driver is using it correctly. Most of the time you can see the driver's eyes in the mirror when they check it. If you see any motion from the back of the driver's head, you take that as a directional. Stay awake and be prepared.

His vision was so concentrated straightforward that the motion of the deer must have seemed like it came out of nowhere. What a rush! You have to take time to understand animals. The deer had no intention of running out into the road. It was running towards its young that were close to the road. All he saw was a deer running out about to cross the road. As the deer got closer, he locked up his brakes. He locked up all four wheels and slid across the road into the car in the third lane. The deer never came any closer to the road than her young and they were of no threat. They were much too happy eating to care. The driver could also have been thinking too much about the car he cut off and considering the other driver's options, might have been trying to drive as fast as he could to get away from the other car. His mind wasn't thinking about what his eyes should have been seeing.

***

We have been working with the threshold of the gas pedal for some time now, and more and more of the students are reporting that they are getting better gas mileage. Little by little, they are finding their pace.

If you ease off the gas and still find that you have to use your brake in a turn, you have to start to ease off the gas pedal a bit sooner and allow more time for your forward momentum to drop. The car up ahead will see a radar trap way before you. So, if the car up ahead hits the brakes quickly, you're easing off the gas and checking your speed as your eyes go to the inside mirror.

Remember…Not getting tickets is the art of common sense.

Chapter 4

STUDENT COMMENTS

I think the one thing that the Driving part of Drivers Ed. helped me to do was check blind spots, drive under stress, and find out how to get home in unfamiliar territory. I also got useful information on highway travel. I was taught how to feel comfortable on the highway, which I couldn't before Drivers Ed.

***

There are many things that I learned in the Driving part of Drivers Education. I learned that "Signals are mechanical and subject to failure." I learned to always watch out for the other cars making stupid mistakes. I should always be aware of everything on the road and off the road. I should drive defensively at all times and not assume that everybody else on the road has taken Drivers Ed. and knows what they are doing.

***

I believe the most important lesson learned in this segment of Drivers Ed. was that of observation, the importance of constantly looking in all directions possible while maintaining one's concentration on the road. Either by looking at the blind spot when changing lanes or in the inside mirror before entering a potentially hazardous situation, or just looking around when stopped. Situational awareness is the most vital part of driving safely.

***

I became more relaxed with driving in general. I saw a great deal more as Drivers Ed. went on. I'm more comfortable with busy areas, braking and highway driving. I notice stop signs, kids and potential hazards. I fear no road.

***

I feel that I have learned a lot about my own driving and driving in general. My wheel control has improved and I also greatly improved my "Scanning ability." I have a better overall view of "The Total Picture" now. I also have a better understanding of other driver's errors.

***

Dear Mr. Myers,
    Drivers ED. was surprisingly good. I have increased my general confidence in all areas of driving. I especially have no problems with getting on highways. I feel positive with my driving and satisfied with the course.

***

What I always heard and finally learned was to check the inside mirror as an automatic reflex.
    What I remember most, To look in the mirror when I stop, wheel control and not to get too close to the car in front of me.

***

Today, I again see progress. A student checked the inside mirror when she brought her foot from the gas to the brake. She never used to check it at all. You have to realize how important it is. I have also noticed that she is driving a bit slower now. She is showing that she is more comfortable with her surroundings. It's easy to do. By expecting something to always be in the mirror, you shorten your reaction time and give yourself more time to think.

When you bring your eyes to the front to check the road, you have to check closer toward the front of the car. I don't mean you look straight down the hood of the car; gaze about ten feet in front of the car. This will allow you to stay in the center of your lane with eyes wide open, while you think about the sound of the car entering your blind spot. You have to check things at least twice to be able to better control the situation.

I was picking up a new group of students today and a former student stopped off to say hello. He had stopped to thank me for telling him about a certain rip-off situation that an unsuspecting driver may experience.

He had had an accident and the place that the car was towed to, informed him that the car was a total loss. They offered to buy the car from him and told him that the car was only good for parts. My former student said no thanks to the idea and instead called his local gas station and had the car flat-bedded to that location. His parents had used that station for a long time and he felt that the owners were fair. They fixed the car in a short amount of time, and he described the amount it cost to fix the car as, "Not much, not much at all. You were right. Thank you, Mr. Myers."

Hearing this was nice. This shows to me a very strong possibility that as this story gets around, the place of business that tried to rip off my student will lose business because of it. He might even lose enough business to consider being honest. He has told all of his friends by now, and when you hear something like this happen, it's your place to bring it to your parents' attention.

Tell your parents about shady dealings that you hear about. You are supposed to get what you pay for, but you might not get what you pay for if you are not paying attention.

Let's get back to class: a student sprang to life in the backseat today as I was explaining that when you approach an intersection, you have to check the end of the yellow line. If the ends of the yellow lines are faded badly, this means that the cars coming out of the road on your right are making the turn too sharp and are going over the end of the double line. They are not going into the center of their lane; instead, they are going across part of your lane. Seeing this faded line situation tells you that you should stop sooner in case this happens to you.

She was totally elated. "I never thought of that," she said. "It's so simple. I was looking right at it and I didn't see it." If there is a stop line in the picture, and the paint has been worn away where the stop line meets the faded yellow line, it becomes easier to detect. If you see this faded line situation, you must be prepared to stop where the color yellow is still strong. You can see that the farther into the situation you go, the greater the chances are of being hit in your front left side by a car that's coming around and across your lane from the right; it's called cutting the corner. These are some of the little things that it takes years to learn.

This is another reason why you must know how close the car is behind you. This will affect your stopping distance. By laying the weight of your foot on the brake lightly for a moment before braking, your brake lights will wake up the driver behind you and get them to start to react sooner.

You have to keep it in mind that no matter how many ways you can find to make your actions understood, some people just don't care.

Some people don't care about themselves and if that's how they feel about themselves, imagine what they think about you. Never drop your guard. Keep your eyes and ears open and think about what you are doing all of the time.

***

Another student came to life today as we were entering a highway. I was explaining that when you are parallel to the first lane and contemplating making a move into the first lane, you can see both what is directly behind you and a good portion of the traffic that is coming up into the blind spot with your inside mirror. It takes a slow glance to the blind spot, a second glance to the mirror, and then a second glance to the blind spot to make sure that nothing is changing from the second to the first. It was clear so we entered the first lane and got into the center of the lane.

I have to stop here and explain that the left directional had been put on way before we had ever gotten close to the road. The directional is put on at the top of the entrance ramp for maximum visual effect. The more your intentions are clear, the greater the chance of entering the highway safely.

Remember…If you can't make a safe move, you must put on your right directional and stop. When there is a space in the flow of traffic big enough to make a safe move, change directionals, excelerate, and enter the flow of traffic.

Remember…if you are watching yourself to catch your mistakes, and correct them now, the chances are greater that you will be able to walk away from an accident. In bad situations, just living to tell about it doesn't make it. After a while, people don't want to hear it anymore. Find your pace, take your time and think safety.

My student couldn't get over how easy it was to enter the highway. He used to keep checking his outside mirror on the driver's door and couldn't judge anything at all. When you know what to expect, it becomes easier to relate to your surroundings. Relax and decisions are easier to make.

More and more students are seeing and what's more important, appreciating, a new approach to driving.

Actions speak louder than words. In the next class, we were approaching an intersection and I told the driver to check his inside mirror and cover the brake and prepare to cross the intersection. We had a green light and we were going straight across. Instead of doing what he was told to do, he asked me why, and kept his foot over the gas pedal. He wasn't pressing the gas, but he didn't move his foot to cover the brake.

You must think of all the possibilities in this situation. Visibility off to the right was excellent, no cars were coming toward us and there was nothing behind us. The snow had been pushed off to the side of the road. This made the width of the road smaller. The corner of the inter-section up ahead sported a very high dirt bank that made it impossible to see anything approaching the corner until they were there. And that's in good weather.

The snow added to the height of the dirt bank so much that it totally wiped out any ideas of spotting the top of the car antenna over the snow. The situation up ahead on the left was totally blind.

We got down to the stop line area and around the corner comes a car making a right against the light. Because of the snow accumulation and excess speed, it swung over the yellow line onto our side of the road. It was head on time. Time to earn my pay.

I reacted and took control of the situation from my side of the car. We were going very slowly when the car came around the corner, so safety and control were not a problem. I had expected this to happen.

Knowing that the student would start to make some long speech about his judgement, I had him ease off the gas a lot sooner so that I could use the small incline to slow the car down more.

I was explaining the dangers of someone coming from the left. He didn't even bring his foot over to the brake. I started to slow the car down from my side and the student seemed to resent my correcting him. I pointed to the corner as the car came around it and he froze: he was frozen behind the wheel. But this could happen to anyone of us at anytime.

In this situation, the student wouldn't listen. I told him right out that if he had been driving by himself or with his friends in the car, that he and his friends would be in the hospital right now. He agreed with my opinion, but still wanted to know how I knew the car was there. I told him to expect friends trying to get back to school before their next class. I told him that for the distance we had from the light and considering the time the light stayed green, it just seemed to me that too many fingers were pointing in the wrong direction. It seemed to me that by the time we got down to the corner, the chances of the light changing to yellow for us were pretty good. The possibility of the light changing increased the threat.

I had been telling him about all of these different things to think, way before it happened; he just wouldn't listen. You have to understand that this experience brought him more down to earth. It opened up his mind for him.

Again back to how did I know. He seems to believe that I really did know that a car was physically there and couldn't understand how I did it. He wanted to know my secret. It's no secret: if you can't see that the area is clear, it's not. It's not clear until you see that it's clear. And even then, you have to expect something to move.

That wasn't good enough; he still thought I had a way that I wasn't telling him. You can have a lot of things going on around you at the same time. When the student didn't cover the brake, I knew I was in trouble. At this point I knew that something was going to happen. Call it deduction or call it common sense. I prefer to call it practicing an open mind, considering my safety first. With his foot over the gas and not the brake, the chances of him thinking brake but pressing the gas instead was excellent.

He froze behind the wheel; most situations go like that because you haven't been driving long enough. You haven't experienced enough different driving situations yet. In this situation it was a lack of common sense. This is why you see if the end of the line is faded and check your inside mirror when you bring your foot over to the brake. And this is why you bring your concentration closer to you after checking the mirror, so you can be in the center of your lane while you think about what you saw in the mirror. It's safety, and what it adds up to is you.

The driver of the other car was a former student of mine and the situation was what it was; the facial expression of the other driver was fear, surprise, and panic. When she saw that it was me and that I had taken control of the situation, a look of embarrassment crossed her face. It was a bad situation that could have become critical and she knew she was wrong. And in the same instant, I saw a look that told me she was glad to see me. I wasn't able to get through to her when she was a student, but I think that hopefully this will take the wind out of her sails.

***

We were out on the highway today, and I noticed that the flow of traffic was going a bit fast. After a good size snowfall, the police have fewer places to set up their radar. People have the tendency to drive too fast for the weather conditions. The police are more involved with accident situations and you can guess why. That's right; it's because some drivers who probably don't exceed the limit often have the chance to get away with driving fast. This is something that has stood out to me for years but it seems to be neutralized by the added amount of police driving in the flow of traffic. The police will work their way through the flow of traffic, they come up behind you and pull you over. It could be an undercover car, or a full dress, lights flashing, scream machine. It won't matter what you say; the officer was directly behind you and you don't know for how long. Think about the situation. Don't make a typical teenage mistake like saying, "I saw you behind me and I was trying to get out of your way." That's the worst ticket to get and the most eye opening. If he/she can sneak up behind you and remain undetected long enough to clock your speed, you deserve the ticket.

Most of the time, we allow ourselves to be distracted by things that we really do have control over. For example, let's take the water that's thrown into the air by the back tires of the car in front of you. I may have mentioned it before; if I did, then you will better understand this next possible situation.

Here you are in the first lane and you are so close to the car in front of you that the water from the rear tires is landing on your windshield. The snow is melting and there is a lot of water running down along the side of the road to the storm drains. If you drift too far over to the right side of your lane, your tires pushing through the water will cause you to experience steering problems. As the front right tire pushes through the moving water, it can cause the car to pull towards the right. The way to deal with that is to grip the wheel tighter and ease off the gas to let the car settle down. Don't forget to check your mirror. A car could pass you in the second lane and put a spray of water onto your windshield while you're fighting the wheel.

There could be a metal grate missing from a storm drain that you didn't see and what we have here are the makings of an uncontrollable situation. Add the element of surprise and you stand a very good chance of doing the wrong thing under pressure. If you stay back far enough to allow the water that's thrown in the air by the car in front to settle back down on the road, you will get little or no water on your windshield. The less distraction you have, the more you can concentrate on road hazards. If these things happened at the same time, the chances of the driver hitting the brake and not checking the inside mirror are excellent.

If you know that a car is passing and it puts some water up onto your car, it's not that bad because you expected it. If that were to happen and you didn't expect it, your reactions will be different.

In the second lane, the water goes off to the sides of the road most of the time. This means the chances of steering discomfort become less. Keep in mind that hydroplaning is a very common thing. You must learn to expect it. Because you can be passed on the left or right at the same time, you can get a spray of water from both passing cars at once. This could cause the driver to freak out. Where are you going to go if you can't see where you're going?

Proper lane positioning is a must because your stability may be compromised by the passing cars. The chances of having, or being involved in an accident, become greater as the weather worsens. The more you stay relaxed, the greater the tendency you'll have to keep in contact with your inside mirror. This is where tunnel vision can really mess you up.

What if you were in the third lane, and probably too close to the car in front of you, so you have more water on your windshield then just the rain. The third lane has a naturally high-speed air about it, like you're in some kind of competition when you're actually not. With you in a speed racer mode and the water running down the left side of the road, all you need is to have a large amount of water come onto the windshield from something passing you in the second lane. While you are fighting the wheel as you go through the water on the left side of the road, the car in front unexpectedly hits the brakes and your reactions are tested to the max.

I am not saying that you are a bad driver; you are a new driver, and I have seen experienced drivers over-react in this type of road situation. Some are lucky and regain control, and some don't. Some drivers hit the brake and take themselves into the guardrail on the left, then shoot back across all three lanes hitting everything as they go.

***

One student had a bit of a problem judging the with of the car today. She couldn't keep the car in the center of the lane. I used the word "today" because every time she comes to class, she has a different problem. Somewhere in the world there are a lot of people who don't have to worry about anything; she's making all their mistakes for them. After I go through the standard explanation, she usually comes down to earth and there is no problem. Today she kept back-talking. I knew I had a problem on my hands.

I knew at that point that if something, anything, were to happen, she would not react correctly. We got off the parkway and pulled over to the safest area and switched drivers. I asked the student that had been driving if the palms of her hands were sweaty and she said that they were, but not as much as before. That is a good sign. Anyway, my new driver put her foot on the brake and pressed hard. Then she started the car and adjusted her inside mirror. The student before her was her size so she didn't have to adjust the seat. Everything was going picture perfect. She rechecked the inside mirror and blind spot and off we went into the flow of traffic without a hitch.

After she found the center of the lane, she checked her inside mirror again. It was perfect; then all hell broke loose. She couldn't stay in the center of the lane. At one point she was all over the road. I asked, "Excuse me, but would it be too much to tell me just what the heck is going on?"

Now she starts to laugh. I asked her if she was laughing because of something I said. The students in the back were showing signs of stress. I told her if she really hated one of the students in the car that much that it would be in everyone's best interests if she addressed her feelings to just the one person in the car and let the rest of us live. She could not keep the car in the center of the lane and it was starting to become, not funny.

She at this point really could not control the car at all, so I stepped in and found a safe place to stop. Nothing was wrong, she said, but something was very wrong. We took time to recompose and went back at it again.

Foot to the brake, eyes to the mirror, so far so good. Out of the park and down the drive, the left directional went on and she checked the inside mirror again. She checked out the blind spot area and with a second glance, we were on our way. Out we go into the center of the lane. And you called it; all over the road we go. After a few minutes of being the fastest man on earth, I decided to pull over and switch drivers. I asked if there was anything wrong with her glasses. She replied, "No, I forgot mine so I borrowed these from a friend." Well, I can't print the comments from her fellow students, but I was happy. The problem was solved.

Author's Note: A car's condition tells you a lot about the driver. If the car is dented, it shows that the driver wasn't paying enough attention. Maybe the driver couldn't help it. Either way, an accident will have an effect on the driver. Usually it makes them wiser. Sometimes, it builds a feeling of false confidences. Accidents can happen very quickly. After it's over, you're shaken and may even experience a loss of direction.

Remember…stay in your car until you have figured out what is really going on around you. The accident might not be over. You might be about to be hit again and not see it coming. Stay in the car and check the situation out before you try to exit. You could live through the accident only to be struck down after exiting the car.

***

A friend's wife was involved in an accident. She was paralyzed from the waist down. I was just told that she has developed some feeling in her feet. That's an excellent sign. I know her; she has three small children at home and more than the will to walk. If she had been wearing her seatbelt, she wouldn't have been hurt so badly. Just because you get older doesn't mean you're automatically going to get smarter. You have to think safety.

***

In a class today, one of the students could not turn and recover using the hand over hand method. I told the back seat drivers to watch him and tell me what he was doing wrong. His problem was picked up very quickly. He wasn't crossing his hands correctly. He wasn't working with the upper portion of the wheel. He was trying to make the turn with the least amount of effort. I told him to work with the upper portion of the wheel more and to try not to make the turn with one sweeping motion. He changed his hands to the ten and two positions and slowed the car down just a bit more. It fell right into place.

Remember…you don't turn the wheel, you work the wheel. His problem started when he copied someone else's poor wheel control thinking that it was right. If your parents and friends have poor wheel control that does not mean that it's the right thing to do. If you copy a problem you get a problem. It's just that simple.

***

Once in a while, an example of what I'm talking about at the time, happens right before our eyes. We were on the parkway. It's a two-lane situation and we were heading north. We had been talking about the turn up ahead and thinking about the cars coming up from behind. As we started to enter the turn, a car passing us on our left drifted too far to the left side of the lane putting the two left wheels on to the trash along side of the road. She was traveling at a high rate of speed.

I had been watching her coming up from behind. We were slowing down entering the turn so we had good control. At the halfway point in her turn, or the apex, it dawned on her then that she was going too fast and she hit her brakes. The turn went to the left, to the right and then back to the left, but at the speed that she was traveling, there was no way she was going to make it. She locked her brakes up and cut the wheel to the right. Her car slid across the road in front of us, then onto the grass and into the guardrail backwards. She was frozen behind the wheel.

When I first heard the sound of the passing car I took control and dropped our speed down even more. I wanted to make sure she had enough room. But she froze at the apex of the turn and that was that. She tried to brake and when she did, her left wheels started to slide on the sand and gravel along side the road. She turned the wheels to the right as she locked her brakes and that was all she wrote.

It was a nice slide, very graceful, uncalled for, but nevertheless graceful. My taking control allowed the students to see the entire situation from start to finish. Because we were slowing down to keep a good distance from the other car; the example was most effective. I was able to talk through the whole thing. I kept slowing down until I saw that the car had not flipped over after hitting the guardrail, then we resumed our speed. There were cars behind us that had already stopped to help. I hoped she learned her lesson.

Remember…once your wheels get onto the sand and gravel that accumulates along side of the road, you have just lost traction on that side of the car. When the wheels get onto the grass, you have a problem.

Remember…if you lock up your brakes and start to slide, ease off of the brake until the wheels start to turn again. Then reapply pressure once again. We don't want to hit anything, but if you do, it's better to be in control.

Remember…most cars have disc brakes on the front and drums on the rear. When you make an emergency stop, the front brakes will lock up first and then the back brakes will lock up. The rear wheels can turn two or so more rotations, after the fronts have locked up. This can cause the back end of the car to come around. This is the start of the total loss of control of the vehicle.

Remember…there is always a chance that a car will hit something and slide back out into or across your lane again. You have to make sure that you have enough control to avoid a possibly worsening situation.

Always Remember…there are two types of accidents. A good accident is the one you walk away from and a bad accident is the one you can't walk away from. You can always buy another car, but what good is it if you can't drive it?

The student driving had been telling me that he and his family had driven all over the place over the weekend looking at different colleges.

He said that there hadn't been any problems at all. Here we are ten minutes into Drivers' Ed. and all hell is breaking loose.

Down the road we went to the traffic circle and a car came out from the right side, ran a stop sign, and cut us off. We knew what was behind us so we were able to stop.

When the situation cleared up, we went about our business. I asked my students if the palms of his hands were sweaty, and his reply was a fast yes. We both laughed at the speed of his reply, because he had always answered no to that question in previous driving classes.

I asked him if the car that slid across the road scared him and his answer was an equally fast yes. So the sweating of the palms is a good sign. It wakes you up to the fact that you haven't reached your full potential yet. That's good; it helps you keep track of your own progress. It's a way of keeping yourself under control.

As the perspiration in the palms of your hand decreases, and this could take awhile in different driving situations, you start to become more self-confident. As a driver, the more self-confident you are, the more you will understand the flow of traffic. The more you know about the flow of traffic, the more you can use it to your advantage.

All of this knowing your surroundings strengthens my theory that you must know what is behind you. Seeing that a car behind you is about to make a mistake gives you time to change lanes or pull over or do whatever you think is the right thing to do to ensure your safety and the safety of your passengers. The idea is to think to see and hear something coming all of the time.

Remember…there is something there. Until you check and prove to yourself that there is nothing there, there is something there, and never forget it.

The halfway point in the turn is where most drivers lose it. You have to check your inside mirror before you enter the turn so you can have 100% concentration in the turn. You must be in the center of the lane when you reach the first quarter of the turn or the rest of the turn is up for grabs so to speak. If you are not in the center of your lane and well in control when you reach the halfway point, or the apex, your chances of not making it out the other side of the turn in your lane are excellent. You could wind up in the trees, against the guardrail, or into the oncoming traffic.

Speed is a problem if there is too much of it. You can always add speed if needed; it's the slowing down part that causes big problems. It's a combination of things: one thing leads to another and you lose it.

Here you go into the turn after picking up speed on a straightaway. You feel the freedom of having, oh, I don't know, total control. I press the pedal and I'm pulled forward. I turn the wheel and I go where I want to go. I can turn my radio up and be cool in my better-than-all-of-your-machines. I can be myself and do what I please with my "I won't take any crap from anybody" attitude. Bad move!

A bad attitude and speed don't add up to safety. You enter the turn faster than you expected and have a problem concentrating on staying in the center of the lane. You make a steering adjustment and find yourself in the center of the lane at the apex of the turn, but you are going too fast. Trying to slow down you'll find that you're concentrating more on not going over the line rather than staying in the center of the lane.

At this point, I would like to welcome you to the three-quarter point in the turn. One of my students prefers to refer to it as "Show time!" You lose track of everything around you because you are staring at yourself getting closer to the line. You know you only need to turn the wheel a little bit to stay in the turn, but because you were not on the correct side of the play in the wheel when you entered the turn, the motion you are making with your hands doesn't make the car move enough in the direction that you need to go. Because you have run out of actions to take, you freeze behind the wheel and hope for the best. Well, that just doesn't make it.

The idea is to get to the three-quarter point of the turn being prepared to accelerate out of the turn. This is control. Entering the turn correctly will get you into the center of the lane at the apex and that sets you up for the three-quarter point and points beyond.

If you feel uncomfortable or you feel your body being pulled across the seat toward the door, you're going too fast and you need to make a speed adjustment before you get much further. If you go around a turn in bad weather conditions and you feel yourself being pulled in either direction as you make it through a turn, you owe it to yourself to smack yourself upside your head a few times until you regain your senses.

If you panic and lock the brakes up, you will slide off the road. If this starts to happen, ease off the brake and let your wheels turn again; try your best to get back into the center of the lane, trying not to over-steer, then reapply pressure to the brake. Or maybe you can steer out without touching the brake at all. Some situations call for acceleration, if this is the case, you must take your foot off the gas immediately after getting back into the center of your lane. You must be familiar with the way your transmission will respond to rapid acceleration. If you press down hard on the gas pedal, it could cause the transmission to shift down a gear. If you are not prepared for this sudden burst of speed, it in itself could cause you to lose control.

Remember…any rapid acceleration will cause the front end of the car to raise up, taking some of the weight off of the front wheels. With a front wheel drive car, this could cause the drive wheels to break traction, creating the beginning of a worse situation. Take your time, keep your speed down and give yourself time to think. You can't let the car get away from you. Drive at a comfortable pace. Don't push you. You are not everybody else. You are you. But to everyone else you are the other driver, so take your time.

***

Today we were identifying objects as we drove along. Most of the students pick it up quickly. One student showed marked improvement in covering the brake. A car started to pull down a drive way to the street. The house was so far back that it would take some time for it to reach the road. It was on the left side and was no threat too us at all.

The driver did not identify the car in motion, but she did cover the brake. When the car got closer to the road, she pointed it out.

This student demonstrated a conditioned reflex and probably didn't even know it. Now I have to get her to check the inside mirror as she covers the brake and we're in business.

I'll start by having her check the mirror every time I say mirror until she gets used to understanding what's behind her.

The two reactions will fall into place by themselves. This particular student was a hard nut to crack but now she's talking and the atmosphere in the car is much better. After they understand that I'm not trying to run them down, their interest grows. It takes time to master the mirror. You can't be staring at the mirror all the time. You have to learn a rhythm and it can never interfere with the driver's judgement.

Say we are entering a long stretch of road with nothing on either side of the road that could be of any threat to us, I'll say mirror. The student checks the mirror. Then as the student checks to be sure they are staying in the center of the lane. They tell me what they saw in the mirror.

If the driver got lost in the mirror, it will show by losing the center of the lane. If you are thinking to see objects that are closer to you first, you will become less confused. The less confused you are, the easier it is to master. Think object, not Ford, Chevy, Chrysler. Don't think blue, white or orange, think object. It's easier. Yes, there is one there, or no, there isn't one there. Think object. Yes or No. This will shorten your reaction time and lengthen your stopping distance.

***

Working the brake is an art. You must know how much pressure to use. If you stop too fast, you could cause a car behind you to hit you. If you don't judge your distance properly, you could wind up hitting the car in front of you. Practicing with the brake is important. The exercise is easy. Find an empty parking lot and put the car in gear with your foot holding the brake pedal down tightly. Then ease the pressure off of the pedal slowly until the car feels like it's trying to start to move.

Press it back down in a slow but firm motion until you feel the car stop again completely. This is called the threshold.

Then you practice letting off enough pressure to let the car move 12 inches. You should be able to do that and feel almost no motion inside the car.

The trick is to not let it get away from you. You must be consistent. Once you master the 12-inch start and stop, stay with it. Don't start rolling up to 20 miles an hour and then stop; the car could get away from you. You must master the threshold first.

When you have enough foot pressure, the braking system starts to work. The tires are the things that make contact with the road and enables you to roll and stop. Without tires, you cannot drive your car.

When you first cover the brake you must know how much pressure you will need to apply to decrease your speed in a safe and timely manner. The only way you are going to learn that is to practice at low speeds first. When you start to feel more control, you can maneuver at higher speeds.

Extra credit was flying around all over the place today. One student's grades went from C to A. You just can't beat self-confidence.

In the winter, you have black ice. Remember that it looks like it's wet, but it is really ice. As the seasons change, the problems change with them. The wet roads with spots of ice turn into dry roads with water on or flowing over them. If you go into a turn and at one point or another the road goes from dry to wet, it could cause you to test your air bag system against a guardrail or in the trees. Your chances of hydroplaning off the road are excellent. If you slide off the road, that's one thing. If you slide into another car, that's another story. This is another reason you never accelerate into a turn. When the road gets wet, you must slow down.

***

On my way to work today, I passed a Beemer being flat-bedded away. I couldn't miss the trooper or the ambulance with the lights flashing, as they went up an entrance ramp toward the hospital.

The car was totaled out. As I passed the truck, I checked out the driver's area. The windshield was pushed out, but not by the driver. It broke, then popped out as the car bent like a tin can, bouncing from tree to tree. There was no blood on the glass or what I could see of the dashboard, so I could guess that the driver had a seatbelt on.

This is what can happen if you are not paying attention to the road conditions. Once you slide onto the grass, your control is greatly diminished. From what it looked like to me, going by the skid marks, the speed was too great for the turn. He started to skid and panicked. He hit the brakes and then locked them up. The car slid across the road went up on the grass and into the trees.

When was the last time you put your seatbelt on correctly? Think about it. The lap belt came into the automotive picture in the early 50's. The shoulder strap was introduced and now finally we have the seatbelt and air bag combination. In the early years of driving, it was thought to be safer to jump from the car. The idea of jumping made more sense than going through the glass windshield and bleeding to death. But times change; today's safety glass and all of the other safety improvements make it safer to stay in the car. Today you are safer staying in the car. Being thrown from the car today is the easiest way to die. You must stay in the car.

When you put the seatbelt on, that's only half of it. The other half is to adjust it correctly. This seems to be a big problem with most of my students. The belt must be pulled tight across your hipbones.

Sit up in the seat; you are in the captain's chair. Sit tall, then pull the belt tight across your hips. You must then take the slack out of the shoulder strap by pulling on it and letting it go. It should come to rest snug across your chest. If the belt rests on your neck, you could put the belt under your collar. They do sell plastic clips that hold the belt away from your neck. If the belt is loose, it's not going to be as effective as the manufacturers intend it to be. So take your time and strap yourself in correctly.

I'm starting to get comments from my students about how their parents are reacting to their constant use of the belt. Going by what I've heard and what I've seen, more parents are starting to put their belts on.

***

Today a parent came over to me after class and told me that she had listened to her daughter telling her about easing off of the gas a bit sooner and that she would get better gas mileage. So she tried it and it works. She told me that it always seemed like she was putting her pocket change into the tank. Now she is amazed at the gas mileage she is getting.

I asked if she was happy with the way her daughter was driving and she came back with an instantaneous, yes. She then went on to add that she was the happiest with the way she changes lanes. That made my day.

Hey, let us consider the possibility of not seeing something. Well, whether we like it or not, the chance is always there. I find that most new drivers do not seem to understand how to judge the speed and distance of other cars. If you just keep your eyes moving, it's easier to determine the motion of the objects in question. It could be a car, a truck, motorcycle, bicycle, skateboard or roller blade and the list goes on.

The first time you check your inside mirror, you think…object, yes or no. The second time you check, you do nothing more than compare the two pictures in your mind. To be good at judging speed and distance requires patience and practice. Keep your concentration close to you and take your time. One thing you have to watch for is starting to stare at an object so long that you start to lose track of the other things around you.

Remember…there is something there, until you check and prove to yourself that there isn't anything there. You must always check more than once and give yourself time to think.

***

Today I stopped at a light on my way to work. Everything stopped very nicely behind me. I had two lanes headed north and two lanes headed south separated by a guardrail. The light changed to green and the car next to me took off across the intersection. I started across the intersection thinking about where the second car was.

Remember…where there is one car there will be another.

I got across the intersection and checked my mirror for the second car. By the way the first car took off, I thought the second would be right behind it but I didn't hear anything.

I located the second car in my mirror. The driver was starting to cross the intersection, folding a newspaper at the same time. The cars behind him started to honk their horns. I could see the driver's eyes go to his mirror as he started to pick up speed. It looked like he was trying to do twelve things at once.

He picked up speed and started to drift to the left side of the road toward the guardrail. I'm watching this now. I have no one in front of me and I should have had a camera. He was so busy trying to straighten everything out on the passenger seat that he didn't notice that he was accelerating into the guardrail.

I watched his left front fender be crushed like tin foil. The car just folded up. The wheel went into the guardrail supports and blew out. Then it was ripped right off of the car. He wasn't even trying to stop. He didn't even try to steer out of it.

When the wheel ripped off the car, the car came to a stop. The car was totaled. This car was beyond repair. The wheel also took out an axle and steering assembly. It ripped the strut right out of the wheel well housing. The car was stuck to the guardrail.

Small cars are a problem. You have to have some weight under you. OK, even stupid mistakes happen and all we can do is our best, but he lost his whole car in one shot. If he had been in a larger car, he would have damaged the fender and maybe the door, but he would have still gotten to work on time.

What if there had been less of a restriction? What if there was no guardrail at all in this situation? Could you imagine starting to cross an intersection and find a car accelerating towards you with the driver folding a newspaper? You know, I keep thinking that I've seen it all but it just never ceases to amaze me.

Remember…if you have to read something, pull over first.

***

Back a ways, I had a student get into the car and tell the others in the car to be quiet. Well today, this student displayed to me his total lack of consciousness. We were making a left turn into a parking lot and the driveway was a very steep grade. A sidewalk going across the driveway created a bigger problem. Your front wheels climb, then go across the sidewalk. The problem is that the sidewalk is flat. As the wheels roll across the sidewalk, the bottom of the car that's still over the bump gets closer to the ground. That is what's called bottoming out. In this situation, you must always take your sweet time. You must go very slowly.

Mr. Football accelerated toward the bump, and hit the bump—we did. I got my foot to the brake and slowed us down some, but not enough. Just slamming on the brakes can cause a bad situation to turn ugly. Accelerating into a situation like this will cause the bottom end of the front of the car to slam into the ground. Most of the time this damage can be avoided.

It is these types of repairs that your parents would find, to say the least, enough of an excuse to banish you from the face of the earth.

This student had an air of excellence about him. After we bottomed out, his air of excellence vaporized. We pulled into the first parking space and switched drivers. He tried to talk his way out of it, but you could see that even though he was talking, he knew he was wrong and the other students told him so.

There is no room for this type of behavior. There was no show of concern for the passengers' safety, or for the safety of the training vehicle. I will not allow a walking ego trip to affect the progress of his fellow students. When you drive, it's for real. Some people take longer to develop an adult personality than others.

Eye contact gives you a better idea of what to expect from other drivers. But, you just can't start staring at people when you're driving. Keeping track of the people around you and their attitudes is a must. This is where eye contact comes into the picture. You have to be on the look out for the actions of others. As a driver, you have to think of things from all angles all of the time.

First off, you can't stare at anything. You have to keep your eyes moving. If you start to stare at one object, you could wind up ditch diving. Some people start to act strange when they think they are being watched. Some might take it as a come-on of sorts.

Watching to see if the other drivers are checking their mirrors and checking to see if they are checking to see you, is a very important thing. You want to know that they know you are there. Sometimes they don't see you.

Remember…you are always ready to sound your horn. Never be afraid to use it.

***

Today we were practicing making left turns. If the traffic is heavy, it might be better to think of an alternate road. You have to wait until you pass the last road on the left before you put your directional on. This way the car behind you will know where you are turning. If you have two roads off to the left and you want to show your interest sooner, you can bring your foot to the brake and apply just enough pressure to put your brake lights on. Then after you have passed the last road on the left, you put your directional on. The same action can be used for right turns provided you have passed the last road on the right before you put your directional on.

We were traveling up a grade and about to pass a bicycle rider who was having a major problem switching gears. He looked like he was going to lose control. This is just another one of the many things you have to look for. You have to watch for them all the time. Always give the rider the room you would appreciate if you were on the bike. It's nice to be polite.

So now we have a bicycle pedaling up a hill changing gears. He didn't seem to be able to find the right combination. We had a double yellow line and traffic ahead, coming down the other way. This is a one lane in each direction situation with a double yellow line on the hill and no sidewalk. We put the left directional on and went as close to the line as we could as we passed. Then the directional went off as we got back to the center of the lane. The approaching car had moved to their right to insure safer passing.

All in all, a perfectly executed maneuver. The mirror and blind spot were checked correctly. All of the added information from the back seat drivers was correct. It was a nice move with good control.

***

In this class, we were getting close to the last road on our left. It was decided that we would press the brake. Then we would put the directional on. If you are going to turn into a road, you put the directional on before the road. If you are not going to turn, then do not put the directional on. Signal your intentions at the right time.

As we started to slow down to turn, the car behind us came right up on our back bumper. At one point, I was going to cancel the move and accelerate forward. It looked like we might get hit.

The car behind us finally started to slow down and it seemed like we were safe again. My guard went up. I told the student to be careful because the car behind us might try to pass. My student started to laugh at my statement. Why would anyone pass a car on the left when it was turning left? Well, he found out different. The car behind us flew around our left side to pass, just as we started to turn.

I took control and canceled the turn; my student couldn't believe what was happening. At first he fought me for the wheel. It was like he was in a situation and he knew it, but he couldn't correct it. This is what we call freezing behind the wheel. A big part of this is taking things for granted. If you take it for granted that its going to happen, you will react in a more timely fashion. If you drive around with the idea that nothing is going to become a challenge, you won't be able to react to the situation in time.

I put my hand on the horn and let it blare as the car passed us. I looked to see what the other driver looked like. He was a middle-aged man. His eyes were straight forward. He knew he was wrong. He was just hoping that he would get through in one piece. He looked like a little kid in grown up clothes. To look at him, you would swear that he had shrunk. He looked like his clothes were three times too big. He was dead wrong and he knew it.

My back seat drivers had more than enough comments to make. After listening to them, I found their basic idea of safety was quite sound but I thought we should stay away from tying people to anthills.

In another class, we were preparing to make a right turn. The switch for the wipers is on the end of the directional and if you put he directional on using the palm of your hand, you will put the wipers on. This happens all the time during the first few weeks. Everyone laughs at this mistake. The further into the course we go the more serious this mistake becomes. Instead of turning the directionals on, she grabbed the lever that adjusts the tilt and the wheel went into the up position. This just about scared the lunch out of her. She screamed and the back seat people went into such a fit of laughter that we had to pull over and stop. It took us ten minutes to recompose.

***

Special note; If it is at night and the roads are wet, sometimes you can see the reflection of the brake lights on the wet road under the car in front of you. This tells you that there is a reason to slow down. If you are paying attention, you can ease off the gas and check your mirror. Most of the time you can get your brake lights on before the car in front of you. This wakes up the driver behind you.

You can't just drive around looking under all the cars all the time. It's just that there are situations where you can see things, and these things are very helpful to you.

The signs: don't forget the signs. If you see a yellow sign with a picture of a traffic light on it, it means that there is an intersection up ahead. You might be able to see it or it's around the bend. What it's telling you is that it is time to start slowing down.

You check to see how close the objects behind you are. This is the start of preparing to stop. The mind is working. It is judging speed and distance. It is your call. Ease off the gas slowly; let the forward momentum drop. Allow the car to reach the point where it's slowing down, and then bring your foot over to the brake, find the threshold and decrease the speed. You've checked your mirror and everything looks great. But what about checking to the left and right when you stop? What if the light does not change and you don't have to stop? You will still have to check to the left and right for people running the light.

If you are prepared to stop, your concentration is closer to you. If you are thinking to drive straight through, you will have a tendency to take right-of-way. Taking right-of-way could cost you dearly.

We study to gain knowledge. This is the process of mental growth. You must be thinking about driving. This next student is not pushing herself to learn. She was demonstrating excellent hand over hand wheel control for the longest time. I kept saying 10 and 2 or wheel control. When I say either one, it means to my students to put their hands on the wheel in the proper position.

Anyway, today I didn't correct her at all. I wanted to check her progress. I had her make a few left and right turns. Her hand over hand wheel control was excellent. But after we straightened out, she dropped her hands from 10 and 2 down to 3 and 9. What she was showing me was the way she held the wheel when she drove by herself, like I wouldn't notice. I said to her, "Excuse me, do you know what time it is?" She read the time off the dashboard clock and went about her business. Her hands didn't move. I said, "Hey, I saw a clock in my neighborhood the other day. It was a big cartoon clock." She said, "Yeah." I said, "You should have seen the hands on this thing. They were five times too big for the clock. The hands were so big that they covered up the 10 and 2 o'clock numbers on the face of the clock. She didn't pick up on the hint at all.

Even with my hints, she didn't put her hands in the proper place on the wheel. Well, what am I to do? I marked her for observation, judgment and control. We'll check back in on this one. Some say that if you have an airbag that you should keep your hands at 9 & 3 o'clock on the wheel, but the correct way to steer hand over hand is to start with your hands at the 10 & 2 o'clock position on the wheel.

***

When I turned on the radio today, the first thing I heard was the weather report. It's going up to 70 degrees. Then I heard that two cars had turned over on different roads in key areas. One on an entrance ramp to a major bridge, the other in the middle of the expressway.

Remember…when the weather gets nice, people get crazy.

My 2:15 class yielded one student. The one that was told the first week by my supervisor, on my request, to either get his act together or come back in the summer. He chose to get his act together, but his driving is not improving. He starts to recover hand over hand and then checks to see if I am watching. He does not understand that he's not doing it for me, he's doing it for himself.

You feel good when you demonstrate proper control. After 10 minutes of playing the role of Mr. Perfection, he started to drive like he normally does in his own car.

As time went on, his speed increased, his braking started to become more delayed and his reaction time was not in the ballpark. I point out things as we go along but most of all, I'm watching him show less and less control. This situation started to look like a direct threat to my safety.

This student has a severe case of tunnel vision. The chances this student would run a stop sign were excellent. The point being that he wouldn't have even seen the sign, then argue that there is no sign. Sometimes you can talk, talk, and talk, but it falls on deaf ears. What can I do?

***

Today, again, I started to see results. Last week I informed a student that if she couldn't show me that she could steer hand over hand and recover by this week, that I was not going to work in some extra driving time for her to practice. This extra driving time would probably put a kink in her after school activities, so that in itself helps to create more enthusiasm. When she drove, she showed remarkable improvement. I told her that she was doing a lot better and she told me that she had been practicing; it showed. She will be good at it. This is called improvement. No extra time needed.

She has also showed improvement when it comes to making turns. When you turn onto a road, you must go into the center of whatever room there is for you to use. Only half the road is yours. If there are lanes, you must turn into the correct lane first.

Remember...you can't change lanes until it is safe to do so.

Remember...you can't touch the end of a stop line or touch the end of the double yellow line when you make your turn. It may look like the front wheel isn't going to touch the line, but what about your rear wheels. The back wheel can't go over the line either.

Remember...when you make a turn, you must go from the center of your lane into the center of the lane.

She is giving the car less gas and is able to control the car easier. She also stopped watching her hand go to the directional. She keeps her eyes moving and seems more relaxed. She kept her hands on the wheel at 10 and 2 position. These are the results I get when the student wants to learn and most of them do want to learn.

I happened by chance to meet a parent of one of my students today. He was very happy with the way his son drives. He said that from his son's description of me, then seeing me standing by my car at school, he figured that it was me and came over and started talking. That's nice. It's what we call feedback. Here stands someone I have never met before wanting to shake my hand. It gives me incentive to concentrate just a bit more on my problem students. It's funny how it works that way, but it does. It reinforces your belief in what you're doing.

***

I stopped to get the newspaper today and the picture on the front page was of a car on it's roof. The doors looked like they had been cut off so the passengers could be removed from the wreckage. Two young people died on lunch break. That's definitely a principal's nightmare.

***

Today, one of my students started to talk about how she eases off the gas pedal more now. She said that it seemed like she was always in the gas station before. If you're getting better gas mileage, you are slowing down. That's not hard to understand and it works. A back seat driver commented that she used to drive up to a turn and then hit the brake. She changed to easing off the gas sooner and letting the car settle down as she checks her inside mirror. It's good to see that they see their own improvements. Both students seem very proud of themselves. They are driving better and they can see it. That's what makes me happy.

When I pulled into the lot today, a former student came over to me. He had just changed a flat tire for a fellow student. I had taught a few classes on changing tires last summer and he had been one of the students. He had a smile on his face from ear to ear. His first solo tire change and it went perfectly. He was proud of himself and he should be. It was a job well done.

***

Headlights, people. Headlights, when it rains. When you put your wipers on, you must put your headlights on. This is not a game. It is the law. Any driver will tell you that as the weather gets bad, the headlights go on. The idea is to stand out as much as possible. If it gets later in the day and you notice 3 or 4 cars with their headlights on, that is a signal to you to put your headlights on. If all of a sudden the sky grows dark and stormy, you must put your headlights on. When driving through a tunnel, put your lights on. Just remember to turn them off when you come out.

Remember…when you walk away from the car, remember to check the front or the rear of the car to make sure you turned your lights out, before you turn your back on the car.

***

Today we were approaching a stop sign when a fast moving four door pops up on the road to our right. It was a four way stop. When we stopped, this car to our right would have had the right-of-way; nevertheless, she showed no signs of slowing down. As it got closer to its stop sign, the driver tapped the brake and that was all. We looked at the driver as she passed through the intersection; she was talking on the phone.

Now, a rolling stop pops up in front of us now and again. They are against the law and shouldn't be done, but she buzzed right through. There was enough pressure applied to light up the brake lights; that's about all. If a person had walked out into the crosswalk, it would have been road pizza time. If it were a little kid, the car would have popped it like a bug.

I said to my students, "Check this out, she's driving right through. I wonder where the police are now." This was no sooner said when a police car appeared to our right and was in hot pursuit.

All of the students in the car had something to say about the other driver. They all had very good points of view, but I think we have to let the tar and feather part go.

My students said that talking on the phone is a distraction when driving a car. The first thing blurted out was wheel control. This made me extremely happy. It doesn't take much to figure out that if one hand is somewhere else, the two hands are not together. Correct wheel control is with both hands on the wheel.

***

It is very bright out today. This means more shadows to scrutinize. As you drive through the year, you are challenged by nature all of the time. Clean your windows; give yourself a break. Check it out. Dirty windows and a bright sun make a bad combination.

Remember…Directionals are mechanical and are subject to failure. They could fail on your car or on any other vehicle on the road. And a car has not stopped until you see it has stopped. And even then, there is no guarantee that it will remain stationary. You must consider the human factor.

On the radio, they just finished talking about the students who were killed on their lunch break. The announcer said that most of the people at the service were high school students. One student at the service told the announcer that it just goes to show that when God wants you, it's your time to go, and you never know when.

That's a nice after the fact idea. Six students in a compact car trying to get back to school without getting caught. This time it didn't work. Two dead, one in the hospital in questionable condition. The rest got cuts and bruises, but will be mentally scarred for life. You have to take care of yourself by thinking to stay out of danger.

Sixteen hundred students showed up at the service. I wonder how many of them cut out of school the next day for lunch.

***

Today was erratic turn day. Making wrong turns and late turns seemed to be the order of the day. Cars in front of us were turning into roads and driveways. We saw one car turn into the curb. The tire blew out and the wheel cover took off into the trees. People were turning halfway into things and then stopping. People were backing out of everywhere. If you hit them, whose fault do you think it would be?

We had a car up ahead that was half in the driveway and half out. The driver didn't seem sure of where he was going, forward or backward. A back seat student asked me what I saw. I said trouble.

I turned the situation into an exercise. I asked for the worst case scenario assessment of the situation and for the best course of action to be taken. The voices all came to life at the same time. Everyone had different ideas. One student said to pass, while another said to stop. In this situation, the safest thing to do was to stop. If we tried to pass and the car backed out into our lane, it could create a big problem.

Remember…if there is an accident, you want to keep it as contained as possible. Flying around something can create a bigger problem.

Looking at the positioning of the car in question, I thought it best to stop. The driver checked his inside mirror and covered the brake. Then he sounded the horn twice, in a polite manner, and we started to slow down. We had been talking about the traffic coming up from behind. What if the car backed out into the road when a car was passing us? Would the driver of the car in the second lane be prepared to react properly?

After we sounded the horn, I said that he was going to pull in. The same voice from the back seat asked again, "What do you see?" I said that I saw an older person in a brand new car. The back up lights weren't on and the driver was trying to sit up as far as possible. This told me that the driver was trying not to hit something. The driver's hands were on top of the wheel in clear sight at all times. If I would have seen the driver take one hand off of the wheel and the back-up lights came on. It would have been a different story.

Remember…when the back up lights go on, the car is backing up. If the driver is thinking about backing out, you can tell by the way that they start to check their blind spots. When we sounded the horn, it told the other driver we were there. The horn lets you be seen. Use it wisely. Keep in mind that anything mechanical is subject to failure. It's up to you to call the shots. The car could be put into reverse and the back-up lights don't go on. Pay attention to the actions of the driver.

Another bad situation to watch out for is the car that slowly drifts to the left side of the lane and then without warning or directional swings a right turn across the road. If you see a car drift from the center of the lane, there is something wrong. You may see a crossroad up ahead and think that because the car in front of you is drifting to the left, that it is going to make a left turn. That is a deadly mistake. You can't know until you see it turn.

***

This afternoon I had two students who just passed their road test. One thought she would never pass. She took the test and did everything perfectly. She was very proud and she should be.

This called for a celebration, so off to the drive-through we go. She is driving first. My guard went up. Some people drive well until they pass the road test, then it's all down hill from there. So, she adjusts the seat and makes sure she can reach the pedals correctly. Seatbelt goes on and she adjusts it correctly. With her foot on the brake, she starts the car. Directional, mirror, blind spot. She put the gear selector to drive, then she brought her foot from the brake to the gas and ran over her first squirrel. There went the Happy Meal.

***

Today we went over a bridge that had just been recently repaired. As we started to drive onto it, the driver smiled a big smile and said, "Look it works, it works." The back seat drivers went up in a fit of laughter. The driver came back with, "Well it could of you know," meaning that it could have collapsed as we went over it.

I gave the driver extra credit for considering adverse driving conditions. This brought an instant negative response from the back seat people. "How can you give her extra credit for saying something so blonde? I asked him if he had thought of it. He said no. Another student in the back seat said, "I thought of it." I asked him why he hadn't said anything, and I got no answer. It turns out that the driver's mother was the first to experience the missing section of the roadway that closed this bridge for repairs in the first place. My driver was correct, she was thinking about the entire structure.

Further down the road, a traffic light burned out right before our eyes. It was the first my student had ever seen and she was quite impressed by it. She kept asking everyone if they had seen it. When we got back to school, she told all he friends that she had seen the light burn out. It caught her by surprise and she will probably talk about it for days. If she talks about it for days, that means that she is thinking about traffic lights. She saw a light burn out and will be thinking to see it happen again. When she approaches an intersection, she will automatically think about the light. It could work that way; I hope it does.

Later, on another road we found ourselves stopped waiting for a car to parallel park. I was talking about knowing what's behind you and watching out for pedestrians coming out from between parked cars. We started to talk about how good the chances were that the now parked driver would open the driver's door into the flow of traffic, and sure enough it did. We sounded our horn and he closed his door. So we went on down the road. Sometimes they will get out whether you honk or not. Some people have a death wish. Some people think that life goes on as normal when you're dead. I don't know what they think. One thing I do know is that in a confrontation between metal and skin, skin always loses.

***

We were on the highway today and up ahead of us we could see a dead deer on the road. A small Bronco was on the side of the road. It had a good amount of damage to the front end. The bumper was bent, the headlight was broken, and the grill was a mess. We got off at the first exit and drove back to see the situation again. It seemed like the driver saw the deer coming out and hit the brakes.

You have to remember that deer are woods smart and not street smart. Once you leave the city, you have to think deer. We put up deer crossing signs in known areas but they cross where and when they want. October through December is the period when the most deer accidents occur.

Remember…Deer change color through the seasons, so you need to think to see them.

Chapter 5

STUDENT COMMENTS

Some things I learned in Driver's Ed are ways to use less gas—like not stepping on the gas when going down a hill, or coasting to a stoplight. I also learned some defensive driving skills such as driving in the first lane so you're further from oncoming traffic. Also I learned to always check in the mirror when stopping and that if you're half way through a traffic light and it turns yellow, it's better to go all the way than stop in the middle of an intersection.

***

I honestly feel I learned a lot in Driver's Ed. My parents both feel it has helped my driving. For instance, I learned how to drive on the highway and I learned which highway goes where. I also learned how to get to different places. I also think it helped it improved my gas mileage. I also use my brake less than before. Overall, I am able to change lanes, go around curves, and drive with more attention better than I could before the program.

***

I've learned to
- Check inside mirror!!!
- I have better gas mileage.
- Be more aware of what's happening around me.
- I feel I understand the rules of the road better.
- I feel more confident in all driving situations.
- I also understand and realize how important hand over hand recovery is.
- I now know that I can name 101 objects while driving.
- I am now an expert in all major drive-throughs (i.e., McDonalds, & White Castle).
- I learned how to drive with some distractions, such as losing my mirror.
- Unfortunately, I still can't draw an accurate map of my hometown.
- I can recognize the mistakes of other drivers
Thanks.

***

As a driver I feel very comfortable with observation since Driver's Education. Every time my foot goes to the brake, I check my inside mirror. I also look from side to side more as I drive and I am more able to see the other cars pulling out at intersections etc.

***

As things went, today we were watching a "Don't make a full stop, just turn on red day." I saw a lot of pedestrians doing the 2-step to get away from being hit by turning cars. One pedestrian got a bit more than annoyed and increased a driver's vocabulary. At another intersection, an older woman was crossing the road and was brushed by a car as it passed her. The driver was wrong. She had the right of way. It caused her to drop her groceries in the street. She started to yell at the driver and the driver stopped his car to answer back.

This was a big mistake: this young older lady meant business. The driver started to get out of his car yelling at this, now-approaching, not-too-happy senior citizen. Before he could figure out what she was trying to say, the older woman hit him upside the head with her pocket book. Then she proceeded to kick him in the shins. The driver was experiencing a form of driver danger: it's called an angry pedestrian.

Judging by my eye contact, there were three people who would have gotten to him before I did. If he even looked like he was starting to think about raising a hand to her, he would have had a major problem on his hands from the general public.

All of this happened right out in the open: nice day, blue sky, mid afternoon, with people everywhere. If there had been a policeman there at the time, he would have had a field day with his ticket book. The police can't be everywhere all of the time; it is your responsibility to give whatever aid you can. This doesn't mean that you jump into a fight and try to stop it. There is information that can be written down; find a phone and call the police.

So, now he's trying to get back into his car to get away, and she's still swinging. He fell getting into the car and drove away while trying to close his door. A passerby called out, "Granny Ali". A store worker came out with new shopping bags.

***

Two students finished the driving portion today. One said that he is using his mirror all of the time now and that his blind spot problems are a thing of the past. The other student called over the back seat, "What about rolling?" This started the driver talking about how he practices easing off the gas pedal and letting the car slow down before a turn and that he has noticed that he doesn't have to use the brake as much as he did before.

Both students agreed that their gas mileage has increased. Both students agreed that their driving has improved and they were happy about it. Self-confidence is the name of the game. The backseat driver commented that since he has been taking Driver's Ed., his parents have been letting him use the car more. It's not just the fact that he was taking Driver's Ed. that got him the use of the family car; it's because he came to class to learn and he did. Your parents are looking to see that you become responsible. Nobody just lends you the car, and when a loved one is involved, it takes more convincing.

Remember that actions speak louder than words.

***

The sun was very bright today and the temperature was in the high 50's. Shaded areas were everywhere. A few students still have a problem with adjusting their eyes to the shade. People have a tendency to concentrate on the more lit areas and disregard the shaded areas.

Going from the sunlight to the shade means you have to concentrate closer to the front of the car as you enter the shaded areas.

Remember…your eyes take a moment to adjust; you must know your human limitations. If you are thinking about what's down the road when you enter a shaded area, your chances of hitting something become excellent.

Your eyes take time to refocus, and you are moving at the same time, but which is moving faster? In the time it takes the eyes to adjust, the car has moved down the road a ways. You can't figure out how far you have gone until your eyes adjust. Here comes the big problem. You have to see everything you can as fast as you can and figure out if it's a direct threat to you at the same time. If you are thinking to see what's up ahead as you enter a dark shaded area, it takes longer for your eyes to adjust. For a split second, you can't account for your surroundings.

Remember…Concentrate on what is closest to you first, and then think your way out.

***

It's a nice day today and everyone is starting to drive crazy. People are tailgating and speeding. Traffic in the faster lanes has increased. The difference is the weather and the weather is changing fast. The sky has become cloudy and it's starting to rain. It's the kind of rain that starts, then stops. It's not raining hard enough to wash the thin layer of oil off the road. This creates a very dangerous driving situation.

After the rain clouds go over, the sky is blue again. People see the blue sky and forget about the road. When you have a little bit of water on the road, it can cause you to skid. It's something like black ice except it's not ice. Oil and water don't mix, especially on the road. If you apply your brakes wrong, it will cause the tire to lose traction and skid. In some situations, you can see beads of water in the center of the lane. That's because of the higher accumulation of oil is in the center of the lane.

Next Class…

We passed a three-car pile up on the entrance ramp. It wasn't affecting the traffic on the highway, but the ramp itself was closed. It looked like everyone was looking in the wrong direction at the same time. One car was into the guardrail and another was in a ditch and the third had spun around and come to rest facing up the ramp. All three drivers were screaming at each other at the same time. Nobody got hurt; it just bruised some egos.

**

Remember…A traffic light has red, yellow, and green lights. If you see the light change from green to yellow, you have to judge your speed and distance from the stop line and know what's behind you before you attempt to stop. Some of my students are still not taking this seriously.

A student was approaching an intersection and the light turned yellow. We were far enough back to stop safely behind a stop line, but instead, the student gave it more gas. I took control of the car and slowed it to a safe stop. As it went, the light turned red before we stopped. A car came flying out from our right side into the intersection and t-boned another car that had passed us to run the light.

A voice from the back seat asked me how I knew it was going to happen. More than enough people had come out to help, so I saw no reason for us to stop. Instead, we went around a few corners and got on to the same road that we had been on. Because of the accident, the traffic was backed up; this made it easier for me to give my explanation.

Off to the right were rows of houses. You could see between the houses. There was a road in front of the houses and we were behind the houses. As we drove along, I had seen a car traveling at a high rate of speed towards the intersection. I could only see the car through the spaces between the houses as it sped down the road. From what I could see, as it got closer to the intersection, it started to pick up more speed instead of slowing down. Because of the angle of the roads, the driver on the side road was able to see our light turn yellow. When our light turned yellow, he picked up speed. He figured that the light would be green for him when he got there and it was. He just took it for granted that everyone else would stop. He could see that we were slowing down, the same as I could see he was picking up speed. This is a good class. They appreciated my observation; then that old statement hit the air again: "I would have never thought of that, Mr. Myers."

Remember…keep your concentration close and allow yourself to see what's going on to your left and right side. By keeping your eyes relaxed, it makes it easier to check your mirror. Concentrating straight forward will cause tunnel vision. If my student had been alone, he would have been hit. If he had been hit, the force could have pushed him across the road into a head-on collision. If this had happened, all of the students agreed he could have wound up dead.

The number of students in a class varies. If there are fewer students, you pick up your driving time faster. In another class, one student wound up driving by himself a few times and knew that he had picked up a lot of time. He was very enthusiastic about it. As the lesson was ending, I started to add up his time. He wanted to know how much he had. It turned out that, due to the absence of his fellow classmates on several occasions, he had finished his driving time and now only had to finish the classroom portion. He was totally flabbergasted; I reassured him that my book was correct. All of my students know that what I put in my book is correct because I explain everything as I mark it.

Now his attitude changed. He relaxed behind the wheel. You could see the difference. He had been fighting the machine. Now, he's sitting in the machine going where he wants to go. He eased off the gas and checked his mirror. Not because I told him to; he did it by himself. That's a conditioned reflex he didn't have when he started Driver's Ed. It's good to see such a display of self-confidence.

)|(∗⁆∗

In a conservation today, a student started to talk about a student from his high school who died in a car accident. The story is that he had a fight with his girlfriend, jumped into his car, and sped off into the night. Somewhere down the road, he lost control. He went off the road and into a tree. He had no seatbelt on. These are the stories I don't like to hear.

Every once in a while you see a scene on television where someone gets mad and starts kicking the car. If it kept them from getting into the car, it might have saved their life. I'm not saying you just go around kicking your car; I'm saying you have to be smart enough to channel your energy in a different direction. That sounds good, but we all react differently in different situations. That is why I put this information together. It's food for thought, so to speak. If you get really mad at something, you must wait until you calm down before you attempt to drive.

***

As my students show progress, I change my routes to introduce them to different problem situations. We were approaching a turn in a not-so-wide road. There were no sidewalks and the bushes came out to the road. The road had a double yellow line. In this not-so-wide situation, there was a pedestrian walking toward us.

My student put the directional on and checked the inside mirror as he covered the brake. He checked his blind spot and pulled to the far-left side of the lane. We weren't going fast and there was nothing coming, so we used a bit of the lined area as we passed. At first, the pedestrian looked like he was trying to find a place in the bushes to get into. When he saw that we were making extra room for him, he relaxed.

After we passed and got back to the center of our lane, I asked my students if they noticed the pedestrian's action after we started to make extra room for him. One student came back with; "He wanted to make sure that there was no car coming up the other way." If another car had popped up, this pedestrian was ready to hit the bushes. If one car were to pass another, there would be no room for the walker. The only room would be in the bushes and he knew it.

Remember…Always be prepared to stop.

***

The trees and bushes become problems in the spring. We were approaching a four-way stop. There was a car to our left approaching the intersection and he didn't seem to be slowing down at all. It looked to me that he didn't see his stop sign. I looked over at the back of his stop sign and sure enough, a big branch was covering the sign.

He crossed the intersection very carefully checking to make sure that we were going to stop. He didn't disregard the stop sign. He drove the situation like he saw it. Judging by his actions, I wouldn't be surprised if he wasn't thinking to himself that there should be a stop sign there. There was a stop sign, but because of the branch he couldn't see it.

This is where the white stop line comes into play. If you see a stop line and no stop sign, that means that something is missing. They just don't go around putting lines down unless they mean something. If you have a line and no sign, that doesn't mean that you have the right of way. This is where your common sense comes into play. The sign and the line go hand in hand. The yield sign is now being fitted with stop lines. Understanding the meaning of the line is easy. Detecting a missing stop sign can be difficult, to say in the least.

At times, if you're thinking for a sign, you are also thinking for the signpost. If you see a post and no sign, that doesn't mean there is no sign. What it means is you don't know what kind of sign was there. They don't just put in posts; they put in signposts. What about the stop signs that have been ripped off of trees? Some signposts are bent down to the ground because of an accident.

***

I had an excellent example of snapping a telephone pole today. This woman I'm sure was not meaning to have her car come off of the ground. She went up in the air and flew across the road. When she touched back down, the pole stopped her.

First off, the 4x4 had snow tires all around. It was set up for rough road and not the smooth surfaces that you are accustomed to. The pole snapped off clean, about two feet off the ground. The top portion of the pole slid down the side of the two-foot stump and remained upright.

All in all, damage was light, considering the situation. I can't help but wonder if maybe the vehicle was in four wheel drive. This can cause problems if the front wheel, or wheels, should leave the road. I drove my students past it to show them what could happen. They all seemed very impressed.

Next Class…I have noticed a bit of improvement in wheel control by my almost-drive-through-the-radar student. He seems to be paying more attention to what is going on around him, and this is excellent.

***

Today, all of my students were using the horn when they were supposed to. In every case, the sounding of the horn by the drivers woke up the other person to a possible bad situation. All of the situations were avoided. This is great, to see drivers taking control of their actions and being relaxed enough to predict potential road problems and avoid them. That's great. These were students who had no idea of driving other than: one is gas, and the other is brake. Now they sit behind the wheel with confidence.

Remember…Don't push; learn at your own pace.

One of my students came to class today with a story about how he was the middle car in a three-car crash. He made a fast stop; the car behind him hit him and he went forward into the back of the car in front of him. He thought because the car behind him hit him, that it was not his fault for hitting the car in front. Wrong. You must leave enough space between you and the car in front. It's their fault for hitting him and it's his fault for hitting the car in front. You have to leave enough room so this doesn't happen.

This is a classic example of stopping too fast, too close, and not knowing what's behind you. If you have someone behind you who is too close to you, you always start to brake sooner. That's the idea of light pressure to the brake first. It's to wake up the driver behind you to your intentions of stopping. He wasn't paying attention and got caught in the middle. There was no damage, but as it stood, he was wrong for being so close to the car in front. I noticed during the driving time that he was leaving a good distance between the car in front and us. I think he learned. Some people don't learn from their experiences; I think he did. From his experience, he also used the mirror more today than usual. It seems being tapped by another car woke him up. It has sparked a new interest in the inside mirror.

As the course goes on, I have each student make a map. Then I give the maps to other classes and if they can follow them, I give them extra credit: and extra credit goes to the mapmakers. When you put the three maps together, it takes us away from school and is supposed to bring us back. We started off just fine. We drove off into the side roads and all the information was falling into place nicely. The second part of the map was easy to understand. It took us across main roads and then headed us back towards school. Everything was going great until we got to the last turn. The map read left turn, but it was actually a right. We were looking at the school at that point, so I felt that was close enough for extra credit.

***

Be careful; Do not place yourself in a bad situation because you allowed yourself to be affected by the flow of traffic around you.

Remember…You are an individual.

We were discussing this as we went along, when up ahead, brake lights started to go on. We slowed down. A car had hit the guardrail and because the bumper of the car was so low to the ground, it went under the rail, hitting the upright supports. The upper portion of the front end went up against the guardrail, totally wrecking the front end of the car. You couldn't tell where the headlights used to be. A perfect example of speed on wet roads; nobody was hurt…this time.

Another one of my students has gotten better at changing lanes. He used to turn the wheel sharply and then have a problem staying in the center of the lane. He has driven this car long enough to know about the play in the wheel. It's an easy motion of the wheel in the direction you want to go. If you make a radical move with the steering wheel when you are changing lanes, it could cause you to lose control.

Remember…if you aren't sure, you do not change lanes. Cars pop up fast and where there is one, there is always another.

One of the advantages of an overcast day is that there is no glare from the sun causing sight problems. The shaded areas are few and far between. There is less risk of hitting something. It's that simple.

Some of the cars around us had their headlights on, so we put ours on. It makes you stand out more. When the overcast is so dense that it looks like it could rain at any moment, put your lights on.

Remember…make sure that your bright lights aren't on. Check the dashboard indicator light. Make sure the brights are off.

When you walk away from the car, you must check to be sure you turned out your headlights. Maybe you didn't push or turn something enough and the headlights went out, but the parking lights are still on. Go back and turn them off. You might as well check and see if all your doors are locked as well. If you got out so fast that you didn't shut the lights, you probably didn't close the windows either. These things are wake-up calls to us. If you go back to the car for one thing, you always check the others.

***

We were approaching an intersection; the student driving has overcome a show-off driving personality. As we got closer, the light changed to yellow. He checked the mirror and eased off the gas. The car will hold the speed for a moment, and then it will start to slow down. At that point, he applied light pressure to the brake to get the brake lights on. He checked the mirror again as he slowed down and then again when he stopped before the stop line. It was done nice and smooth, perfectly executed. A welcome change from when he first started the course.

We have walk and don't walk signs at many intersections. Not all of them work correctly; this is a mechanical impossibility. Things do break you know. The bright side is that most of the time they are correct.

Think of it this way: the walk, don't walk lights control the flow of pedestrians. When the traffic light is about to change, the crosswalk lights go into action to warn the crossing pedestrians to clear the road.

If you are facing a green light, the cars to your left and right are looking at a red light. Because their light is red, the light on the crosswalk in front of them is green. You have a green light, so the walk lights controlling the people crossing in front of you are red.

So if you are paying attention, and happen to see these walk lights start to flash, you can judge your speed and distance and prepare to slow down sooner. Now if you are close and the walk light starts to flash, that doesn't mean you stop your car. They control the pedestrians and the actions of the traffic lights control you. You will be surprised how many more pedestrians you will see.

Running a yellow light is no joke: it's bad business. Big brother may see you run that light and give you a very expensive ticket as a reminder of society's disapproval. When the yellow light goes on, someone might jump the light. Someone jumping the light could happen at any time; but the chances of it happening on a yellow light are much greater.

I saw a car running a yellow light one time. The driver saw the other car and just kept coming. I could see that the one driver knew that the other driver was there. As they got to the intersection, the driver in the wrong just stared straight ahead as if everything was going to be all right. He acted like the other car wasn't even there, or as if he knew the other car would stop, go away or disappear. You do not know who is driving the other car. People make some stupid mistakes. Little things like noticing the walk lights and easing off the gas for maximum efficiency can make your driving more enjoyable, safer and less expensive.

By all rights, in the situation that we were in, my student should have come off the gas sooner than he did. What he did in the situation was all he knew to do and it was done well. Now he has another way of thinking about it. After my explanation, my student said that he would have never thought of it. He said that he saw the crosswalk lights, but that was it.

At the end of the lesson, the student said, "Thank you, Mr. Myers." That is always nice to hear. Everyone's ego needs a boost once in a while. It's good to see results. He will tell his friends about it as you will tell yours.

***

Another student passed her road test and had a funny story to tell. She did a lot of things wrong, but she must have done enough good things to balance it out. During her test, she never stopped talking. To hear her tell it, the inspector didn't know if she wanted to pass her or not. She said that she couldn't turn hand over hand to save her life. She parked five feet from the curb the first time but the second try was perfect. She was able to back up straight 40 feet with no problem. That might have made the difference, but I think we will keep practicing hand-over-hand for a while.

***

With bright, clear days, come sunglasses in all different shapes and sizes. Sunglasses on a gray day are not needed. It depends on the cloud cover and how fast it's moving. If there is rain in the forecast and the sky is very cloudy, I mean there is no blue in the sky to be seen anywhere, you have to check the drivers in the cars around you. See if anyone else is wearing sunglasses. If you find yourself defending your decision to wear sunglasses, you may be in an A type personality mode.

If you check around and find that there are very few people with sunglasses on, you should take your sunglasses off. If you see this situation and you take off your sunglasses, this is correct. This action is a B-type personality. You get the public's opinion and match it with your own.

An A-type personality wouldn't have even thought of it to begin with, or they may see themselves standing out in the crowd by keeping them on. You can't tell what people are thinking; you have to expect a mistake to be made. If something is obviously the safer thing to do, you do it.

In another class today, a student told me that she doesn't grab the inside of the steering wheel anymore and she was proud of it. She should be. This is great. She did have a bad problem with her wheel control. Now she is very happy and quite good. Her hand over hand is excellent.

***

Today seemed to be parallel parking day. Usually you have cars pulling away from the curb here and there, but today it was like someone fired a starter pistol. Three cars that were parked in a row decided to pull away from the curb at the same time. The first car started to pull out and couldn't clear the parked car in front of it, so it stopped. The second car started to back up to give the first car more room. The third car starts blowing its horn to tell the second car that it was getting too close. The first car backs up then pulls out of the space. The third car is halfway out into the road, but it doesn't have the room to get past the second car, so it backs up.

By this time attitudes were getting a little moody. Another car coming down the road pulls up and starts to park in the first car's space. The second car pulls out and around the car that's trying to park and takes off down the road. Another car coming down the road tries to pull into the now vacant second space cutting the third car off.

Now we have a car half-backed in and another car half-pulled in and the third car half-pulled out. It turned into a shouting match. The driver of the third car started to get out, so as we got closer to this comical situation, I told my students to make the next right turn. I didn't want to get caught up in the mess up ahead.

If more than one car is leaving the curb and you happen to be one of those cars, it is in your best interest to let the other drivers around you finish before you make your move. Sit for a minute; wait until things have calmed down before you pull out. An A-type personality would pull out causing problems, or maybe getting hit in the driver's door.

Seeing the situation, the B-type personality would check the seat adjustment and correct it. The seatbelt would be readjusted. You have time to check yourself out. Readjust the inside mirror. Make sure that all drinks are secure and away from your lap. There is always something to do.

***

As a driver, the weather affects you directly. If you have snow, and then it melts during the day and finds its way onto the road, the colder temperatures at night cause the water on the road to turn to ice. Dangerous conditions appear. "What time is the sun coming up?" This is a good thing to know. If the sun comes up at 6:00am and you leave for your destination at 6:30am, the sun has not been up long enough to melt the ice that formed overnight. Ice that forms in the shaded areas takes longer to melt. You must be aware of the situation that you are about to drive into.

Remember…black ice or glaze ice means the road may look wet when it is really ice. Take your time. Listen to your first thought: safety.

Remember…in some areas the water may run across the road due to high volume or poor engineering. These icy conditions can cause multiple car accident much faster than your best reaction time can handle.

The best comparison would be wet leaves. When the colors of the leaves start to change in the Fall, it is time for you to slow down and bring your total concentration closer to you. Wet leaves are bad news to every driver. As you drive along through the years, you will find that the different seasons bring different problems.

Remember…The tire is best effective when it makes good contact with the road. Anything between the tire and the road could cause a skid.

If you adjust your driving habits in the fall by slowing down, your transition into the winter is easier. Know the roads you are going to use by name. Listen to a good news channel in the morning instead of music. Be prepared to leave for your destination. Keep track of your fuel level. Get gas in the daytime. Never plan to get gas in the morning; it changes your frame of mind. Seeing all the traffic going on around you while you are pumping gas may cause you to push yourself a bit when you start to drive, maybe drawing you deeper into the flow of traffic than you normally would be, turning an easy drive into a nervous situation. You get used to a rhythm; once you break the rhythm, it's hard to adjust. Because of your delay, the flow of traffic you enter may be faster and more congested. This has a direct effect on a driver's attitude, judgement and control.

***

One of my students was involved in a accident this past weekend. She was hit by another car, but I don't know whose fault it is yet. She suffered a broken collarbone, various bruises, and some stitches. From the information I can put together, I am inclined to believe that someone fell asleep at the switch so to speak. She must have had her seatbelt on, or she would have gone through the windshield. I am very interested in how the other driver is, the road conditions, right of way, and all of that information. Most of all, I'm glad she is all right. I'll get the story when she comes to class.

In the next class, one of my students who has no permit and has only driven with me, asked in a round-about way how she was doing. She wanted to compare herself with the permit and licensed drivers.

Now I found myself in a bad spot. This student is not just good; this student is great. I can't tell her that out of all my students she is the best without taking a chance of starting her on an ego trip. She has done nothing but pay attention to everything that I have said. She handles a car like she has been driving for years. I taught her to parallel park and how to make a broken U-turn in one lesson, and she remembered it. Getting on and off the parkway is a pleasure. She checks her mirror and blind spots like clockwork. She doesn't challenge anything and in the same respect, she has demonstrated an uncanny ability when it comes to knowing her limitations.

She always has a smile on her face and can laugh at her own mistakes. She is going to take her road test later today and she is nervous about passing it. I told her that I think she will do just great. Then I changed her grade to an A; she liked that idea. I like working with people who like to learn.

We had some rain fall this afternoon and it's supposed to freeze tonight. Tomorrow morning, the roads will be iced up everywhere. Traveling in the morning will be a problem.

***

It was another good day today, directional's were being used more often and I'm starting to see more students checking their inside mirror when they put the directional on. Your eyes are quick, but if you don't know what to think for, you'll miss something.

I only have a few drivers left who must have their foot on the gas or the brake. Almost all have developed the knack of easing off the gas pedal slowly, then after a pause, bring their foot to the brake. The difference between this and covering the brake is that the foot doesn't go to the brake immediately. When you cover the brake, your foot is brought over to the brake pedal area immediately. Covering the brake is a preparation to stop. Easing off the gas pedal slowly allows the car to roll for a distance; then the brake is casually applied as needed. Don't forget to check the mirror.

When judging your speed and distance from a turn, you ease your foot off the gas slightly and check your inside mirror. You allow the car to slow down by itself before you enter the turn. Most of the time, you won't have to use your brake, though you are always ready to brake when necessary.

Remember…It takes time to know your car.

***

My student with the broken collarbone showed up at class today. I've heard a lot of different stories and now its time to get the real story. It goes like this; she was driving down a road toward a stop sign and there was a road entering from the right. A stop sign and line controlled the road that entered on the right side.

Remember…intersections are killers; always proceed with caution.

My student told me that she saw the car approaching through the bushes.

She did cover the brake. She checked her inside mirror too. One goes with the other. Anyway, the car on her right started to slow down so my student thought that it was going to stop. That is a big mistake. A car has not stopped until you see it stop and there is no guarantee that it will remain stationary. Needless to say, it didn't. She had dropped her guard; that's it in a nutshell. She didn't think to see what the other driver was doing. She could have sounded her horn or made a right into the road to avoid the accident.

Remember…one of the advantages of the winter is that leaves fall off the bushes, so you can see cars approaching with ease.

***

Today was bright, clear and warm. People had their radios turned up loud and everybody was a better driver.

That sounds good, but it's far from the truth. Everybody was speeding and tailgating. The faster cars became a big problem in the flow of traffic. One pedestrian was hit at a local intersection. He was in the guarded crosswalk when a driver made a right on a red light, thinking it was green. As we drove by, we could hear the driver telling someone that the sun was on the light and he thought it was green.

I asked my back seat drivers what they thought of the situation and they said the driver was wrong. The light might not have been able to be seen, but the pedestrian could be seen clearly and was in a guarded crosswalk. The pedestrian had the right of way. Another comment was: "How could you just make a turn when you don't know if it is green or not? If he couldn't see what color it was; he should have assumed it was red." Good answer.

***

Today, you name it and it was happening. Cars with no brake lights were popping up now and then. The police were having a field day. Spring fever has a direct effect on your driving.

Sunlight may cause a glare that may cause you to squint your eyes to see better. You might consider sunglasses. If you wear glasses, you can buy clip on sunglasses. Make sure the sunglasses you buy are 100%

U.V. filtering lenses. A good way to check sunglasses is to put them on your face and look at an object across the room, then raise and lower the glasses in front of your eyes. If the object that you are looking at seems much closer with the sunglasses on, don't buy them.

***

Today we saw a teenager pulled to the side of the roadway by a parkway policeman. The car had tinted windows. You can tint your windows to a degree. If you double the tint, then it becomes a problem. First off, you cannot see at night. Changing lanes becomes a big problem because you can't see what's there. The tinted windows also allow the police to sneak up on you without warning. If you think about it, the police are up and down the roads all day long. They know what they see. If you stand out, you make their work easier.

***

Today one of my students said he would like to work on his lane changing. He said that he has a problem checking his blind spot and staying in the center of the lane at the same time. We got onto the parkway and started to practice his lane changing. After a few lane changes, I realized his problem.

After you check your blind spot, you must bring your concentration to the front of the car. Then raise your eyes to see better what's going on, as you think about what you saw in the blind spot. Then get a second glance to be sure that what you believe to be true is really true before changing lanes. He picked this up right a way and was surprised how simple it was to correct the problem. If you are looking far up ahead, then you check your blind spot, when you bring your eyes front again, if you're still trying to see up ahead and you are thinking about what's in your blind spot at the same time, you will not be able to stay in the center of your lane. Keep your concentration close to you.

Take your time; if you push it all together, you will become confused. Learn step by step until you memorize the things to do in their proper sequence. Practice is to your advantage. Driving is new right now and you want to avoid making mistakes. If you don't know, ask. There is nothing wrong with not knowing something; it's when you don't try to find out, that's the problem. One of my students didn't know what a flashing red light meant so she went to drive through it. I took over and stopped the car. If you have a flashing red light, it means that you must come to a full stop, and give right of way to the car to the right. If you are confused, let the other car go first.

The last few days we have had a lot of rain and the grass alongside of the highway is not a smart place to pull on to change a tire. The ground is saturated and the weight of the car will cause the jack to sink into the mud. We passed a driver trying to change a flat tire. His problem was trying to get the spare on. The jack started to sink into the soft ground. He had the jack up as high as it would go but it wasn't enough to put the spare tire on. This motorist was not a happy camper, to say the least.

We had been practicing getting on and off the parkway, so we passed this situation a few times. Each time we went by, the tire changer seemed to be getting more and more annoyed. The last time we passed him, he had fallen in the mud trying to reset the jack. This guy was covered in mud. It looked like he just wanted to sit down and cry. I told my students to watch him to be sure that he didn't throw anything in a fit of anger. As the words were leaving my mouth, the guy jumps up and starts kicking the side of the car. He turns around with a lug wrench in his hand like he's going to throw it and falls flat on his back in the mud.

Well, let me tell you something. I am not one to find humor in the tragedies of others, but after seeing that, I couldn't stop laughing. If some one had filmed it and sent it to a contest, it would have won first prize. I went by about one-half hour later and he was gone, so somehow he must have gotten it together. This is something you don't let happen to you. If you have a piece of wood, you might be able to put it under the jack to keep it from sinking into the soft ground.

***

We were practicing bringing our concentration closer to ourselves, after exiting the parkway today. One of the exits bought us out onto the main road with an intersection up ahead a ways. I asked the driver to check out what he saw, then I asked him to tell me the first thing he saw. His answer was that he saw his hands on the wheel first. That was the correct answer. Coming off the highway, you have to bring your concentration closer to you. On the highway, you have the tendency of letting yourself try to see too far up ahead. When you get off the parkway, you must make sure that you drop your speed to the posted speed limit and concentrate even more on the things closer to you. It's like driving into a pop up target range. If the driver had told me that the first thing he saw was the intersection, I would have had some correcting to do.

I started to talk about not buying gas from a station for at least 24 hours if you see a tanker truck delivering gas to the station. A voice from the back seat asked, "How can you tell." Well, you can't tell unless you see the truck in the station. We went around another turn to find a tanker truck in one of the gas stations up ahead. A lot of these things we take for granted because we know about them but to a new driver, these little items are of great importance. Adding gas to the tank in the ground stirs up sediment.

***

We were driving down the road in class today, when a car up ahead on the right side, started to pull away from the curb. I told my student to cover the brake and to sound the horn. She did and the car stopped pulling out. After seeing the car stop, my student brought her foot back over to the gas. My guard went up and I covered the brake. Before I could give my driver a full explanation of the possible dangers, the car on my right started to pull a U-turn in front of us. In the excitement, my student reacted by pressing her foot down. The problem was that she had brought her foot from the brake back to the gas. She was thinking to stop but she put the gas to the floor instead. I stepped in and took control, stopping the car. The back seat drivers nearly came out of their skins. When you are passing a situation like this, it is in your best interest to keep your foot over the brake until you have passed the problem completely. She learned a valuable lesson today that will stay in the front of her mind for a long time. When you think it won't happen, it does.

***

After coming to a full stop, the driver turned to me and said, "Did you see that Mr. Myers?" "See what?" I asked. "I'm checking my inside mirror when I stop." Then she says that she thinks she should get extra credit for her improvement.

Well, that's not what extra credit is all about but this young lady was hell-bent on getting extra credit. So I opened my book and gave her five extra points. The students in the back seat started to complain. Checking the mirror is something that you are supposed to do all of the time and should be a conditioned reflex. I told them that everyone learns at a different pace and that rewards are decided upon one's individual accomplishments. They didn't want to hear that, but it made sense. Now she starts to drive like she is king of the road. I knew that she had been checking her mirror for weeks now; I had it marked in my book. She thought she was getting one over on me.

Words started to fly back and forth between the students. The driver seemed to be gloating and the other students didn't appreciate it. As we stopped at the next intersection, the driver again turned to me and asked if I'd seen her check her mirror. I said yes then put my foot on my brake and opened my door. I asked her if she could point out the stop line to me.

Her mouth dropped. She had stopped over the stop line. The students in the back seat were quick to comment on her poor judgement. She was so busy defending her extra credit that she dropped her guard. As extra credit goes, if you get extra credit and then pull a dangerous action, you lose the extra credit. Then I mark the mistake and all of the possible hazards that the dangerous action could have caused, including scaring the birds.

I opened my book and played like I was looking for a new pen. The back seat drivers were eager to help me select my corrections.

The more things I mark down, the more explanation I can give, so I mark as much as I can. Then we talk about the mistakes. You can have a bad day or good day. If I mark something in the book and as we go along, I see you're correcting it, I mark it out of the book.

I marked the driver for a stop sign, stop line, speed on approach, poor braking, attitude, judgement and control. That would be a standard call for this situation. Then I marked the students in the back seat for attitude. At first, there was quiet; then one back seat driver asked why. I told them that they might have distracted the driver by having a conversation going for long after it should have ended. Having the driver defending herself over her shoulder to three other people made it difficult for her to drive.

At first there was some mumbling but then they reluctantly agreed that they could have broken her train of thought. This is a good group. They didn't know each other when they started Driver's Ed.; now they hang around together after school. They always come to class with a smile on their faces and they always say goodbye when they leave. One young lady didn't talk at all when she first started Driver's Ed. Then for a while you couldn't shut her up. Now she fits right in with the group.

At 16 and 17, you can find it hard at times, especially if you're trying to prove yourself and find yourself at the same time.

***

We rounded a bend to find ourselves facing two big "Do Not Enter signs". There was nothing coming out of the one way street. Either way, we couldn't go into it; we had to make a right. My student looked at the signs and proceeded to drive into this "Do Not Enter" situation. Big as they were, Mr. Football hadn't seen them. Now he tries to save face by telling the back seat people to shut up. That didn't work: it didn't scare them: one threatened to stick her tootsie pop in his ear.

***

The snow has melted away and new problems become visible. When a black-top road is in need of repair, it's patched. The patches take a beating when the snowplows go over them. This is a situation that is corrected when the road is ripped up and then re-paved. It's not practical to be ripping up the road every time a spot has to be repaired. Black-top is put into the hole and it's packed down tight. Sometimes they last a long time and sometimes they don't; it depends on the amount of traffic that rolls over it.

If you have a problem in the road by your house, call the proper road repair authority for your area, and bring it to their attention. A big wash-out starts somewhere. You've got a responsibility; you might even call it an obligation to society to report critical situations. Water can undermine the roadbed causing water and sewer line damage.

You try to get around puddles when you can. The main problem is that you don't know how deep they are. It could be a small accumulation of water or a hubcap flinging, tire blowing or axle-bending, awakening.

A front wheel drive car stands a better chance of taking axle damage. When you approach a water problem, check out the car in front of you. Watching the wheels of the car in front going through the water will give you a better idea of how deep the water is. If you see a break in the road and there are a lot of stones all over the place, maybe even a few larger rocks here and there, this tells you the wash-out is deep.

Check as you approach to see if there are any wheel covers alongside the road just past the wash-out. If you see one wheel cover or chrome wheel ring along side the road, slow down before you roll through the situation.

Remember the impact wrench? Now might be the time you may not be able to get the flat tire off of the car because the lug nuts are too tight. Keep track of how repairs are done. Changing a tire is not a big job but if you can't get the tire off and the spare was stored with a valve extension on it, you may wind up with a real tale to tell about the time that you didn't make it home until morning. If you're lucky, it won't be raining cats and dogs but it probably will be. This is where your umbrella will be greatly appreciated.

Remember…The misuse of the impact wrench can cause you problems down the road.

***

One student in class showed marked improvement in wheel control, another is mastering the art of lane changing. One at a time, I am seeing improvement.

Then there is always one who has a problem doing things right. He wants to do things right but it just doesn't seem to work. He thinks that he is doing it right, so he doesn't listen. He means no harm; he just doesn't listen. After I point out what he did wrong, he'll go around the block and make the same mistake again. I asked him if there was a passage blocked between his ears and the spark of thought he knows as brain. Now he tells me he is listening to every word I'm saying. When I heard that, my guard went up. When I have been teaching safety for months and a student still thinks to choose his own direction, only time will show him the best direction.

***

Today I gave my students destinations that they were to get to by themselves. The first class drove off into the sunset. They had no sense of direction. We wound up on the other side of town. In the second class, the first student drove around in circles. The second student, who was positive he knew where to go, also drove around in circles. By this time, the third student is telling the driver that he's an airhead and is too stupid to listen. It was funny.

The driver goes to make a right and the third student tells him to make a left. He makes the right and finds it to be the wrong direction. The third student tells the driver that he doesn't know what he is doing and they start throwing insults back and forth. These two students are brothers so it's funny to hear them when they get going. Neither one will admit he is wrong, but at the same time they get along well.

So, we're driving along with the brothers exchanging ideas and I hear over my shoulder, "We're a lab test." The young lady sitting behind me, who is now holding her own with the best of them, says that we were like being in a laboratory. I started to laugh and that caught her off guard. She asked why I was laughing. I told her I was glad that she finally figured it out. This is your rolling laboratory. It's the study of how to get along with people safely under adverse driving conditions. The bad driving condition part is not always the weather; the attitudes of the drivers around you pose a constant threat.

This is my phone book student. She made a face leaving the class. This shows me she understands; sometimes it takes longer for some students to come around. When they do, I'm ready to teach.

***

In one class today, a student told the rest to keep quiet when he drove because he wanted to learn and that they were distracting him. Well, my guard went up with that statement. As a teacher, I took his statement at face value; my common sense told me to expect something.

Another student was given a destination and drove to a location she had been last Sunday with her parents. It wasn't where we wanted to go, but it's a great start. She was there once and found it again.

Remember…when you pull to the curb and stop, you must leave your right directional on. All this week, I've been marking students for not using their directional correctly. It's not "Please use your directional," it's the law! You must indicate your intentions.

Remember…don't copy other people's short cuts. If you learn a short cut, you may never learn the procedure you're shortcutting. You have to learn the guidelines first. After mastering the guidelines, you will find ways of controlling the situation to your benefit. This is where the result should be a calculated advantage. A shorter route between two objects; hence the expression, "Short cut."

***

Today we were pulling away from the front of the school when a former student waved for me to stop. I pulled over and stopped. She came running over to the car to tell me that she hadn't had an accident and she hadn't gotten any tickets. Her face glowed with pride. She is graduating this year and plans to go to college. She seems very interested in going. I asked her what college she was going to and reminded her to check the security at said college. Carrying a whistle with you all the time for security tells you that it would be best to consider another college.

One of my students had parked his car and went into the store. When he came out, he found that his car had been hit in the rear. He brought it to class to show me the damage and ask my opinion of how to repair it. If he put in a claim to his insurance company, he was afraid his rates would go up higher. It wasn't that bad, a well-placed sledge-hammer and a used trunk lid would correct the problem in no time. I showed him what to do and explained how to bang it out with a big hammer and a block of wood.

During driving time, I showed him where the junkyards were in the area to make it easier for him to buy parts. Next week, I'll see how far he got. If he takes his time, it should look all right.

***

Mr. Football finished today. He has relaxed and has stopped fighting the wheel. He uses his mirror more now. His speed is under control; his lane positioning is good, and he is covering the brake and using the directional. The main change was his attitude; his attitude is very good now. He has mastered the art of hand over hand wheel control. Lane changing and blind spot problems have become a thing of the past. All in all, I am very happy with his progress. When I told him that today was his last day driving, he didn't believe me.

Three young ladies in the 4:15 class can talk their way through parallel parking and broken U-turns. They are good, very good. I wish I had more students like these; they like to learn. It's fun to learn. There is so much knowledge around you that you can't comprehend it all in a lifetime. People waste time arguing instead of listening. When you start to listen, you'll learn.

***

Today the weather kept changing all day. First, we had a very nice day, then a not so nice day and then back to a nice day. The weather didn't know what it wanted to do. The flow of traffic was moving very fast today. The traffic on the highways was extremely heavy. There was an accident on the entrance ramp to a major bridge that caused big problems. A tractor-trailer has turned over on another highway spilling its load onto the roadway. What a mess! I've seen my share of these kinds of situations and I can honestly say this was not one of a kind.

There are delays on all the main routes, some because of accidents, others from the high volume of traffic. The news helicopter just reported a head on collision at an intersection. It's a bus and a car; the announcer just kept saying over and over, "The car is really wrecked," like he never expected to see so much damage. What do you think happens when you have a head-on collision with a bus? Do you think your bumper will pop out again? It'll pop out again all right, right out of your trunk. You won't just drive away.

***

The sun visor is not a storage area. Store items in the glove compartment. When needed, you pull the visor down and push it forward all the way to the windshield, then draw it back towards you until you reach the required shading.

If you pull the sun visor down on an angle towards your face and you get thrown forward, it will catch you across the bridge of your nose. If the visor is in the forward position and you are thrown forward, the visor would become a kind of padding between the top of your head and the car. I explained this procedure to a student and he was amazed. He said that he would never have thought of it. Now I know this student will talk to his friends and feel good talking about something that they didn't know.

This is good. It allows the student to dominate a portion of the conversation, where they normally may not talk at all. Driving is something everybody says they do well, but some do not realize the depth of the subject.

***

A truck passed us on the highway today and I told my student to wait to be positive that the truck had passed us safely first. Then he was to put our headlights on, then off, pause, then on and off again. The back seat drivers knew that we were signaling the truck that he could come over. The student driving didn't know what we were doing. One back seat driver told him to watch the back of the truck; after it finds the center of the lane, the truck driver signals 'thank you' by putting his lights on and off. This student learned something new today. He was very surprised that he could communicate with the other vehicle in that manner. At night, it's off then on. No brights. The bright lights will shine into the driver's eyes; this action may cause you both to experience distress.

Today the traffic was moving along with no problems. I'm sure there are problems somewhere, but I had a great day. When you travel, you must deal with the tractor-trailers in the flow of traffic.

A tractor-trailer is designed to carry large amounts of practically anything just about anywhere. Working with a highway situation, you try to fall in with the truck flow of traffic. You make good time because of the consistency of keeping the correct pace. Because of the weight factor, you must pick your speed up just before you start to go up a hill. This action is like throwing the weight of the car at the hill. You use up a lot more gas to get to the top when you start to slow down halfway up.

If you have a full tank of gas and people in the car, it may require more acceleration sooner to enable you to hold a comfortable speed to the top. You pick up speed; then easing off the gas as you get close to the top.

Because of the weight of the tractor trailers, the driver will pick up a lot of momentum to insure safe passage over the top. If a truck comes up behind you very close at about three-quarters up the hill, you might be going too slowly for the situation. You should have anticipated it. Your fault! Maybe you could change lanes and let him or her roll by. Sometimes you pass a slow moving truck going up a hill. That means you'll have a fast moving truck behind you going down the hill.

Remember…they have a destination and the driver intends to be there on time.

It is hard to realize how to apply the rules of the road if you don't know how the system that the rules apply to really works.

This is the last week. The handshakes, the hesitating to go and the hug when I wasn't looking. None of this can be put into words. These are feelings that must be felt in order to be appreciated and they were all very much appreciated.

Thank you for the T-shirts. One of you still owes me a quarter. The next few pages are student comments.

I wish them all the best.

STUDENT COMMENTS

I feel so much more comfortable than when I started Driver's Ed when I enter a highway. I speed up to enter traffic smoothly. Also, I am no longer afraid of the narrow passes on the parkway. Thirdly, passing is better and easier than it was.

***

I learned:
- 10 & 2
- using my rear view mirror
- how in general to be a safe driver
- when to use directionals
- how not to drive on the yellow line when turning
- how to make better turns
- how to be more aware of cars, people, etc.
- how to put up with the other 2
- how to come to a complete stop
- how to change lanes
- and everything else I know about driving.
    - Hand over hand recovery
    - Checking mirror before stopping
    - Passing
- Less tunnel vision
- More comfortable driving
- More comfortable w/ highways
- Anticipating other people's actions

***

I learned how to drive. I have learned to be more aware of things and people around me when I'm driving. I learned how to manage gas mileage and be a safer person to drive with. I feel I have better control of the car than when I started and can deal with situations as they arise. Basically, I have increased my driving ability by 101%.

***

The thing that helped me was when you said to look through the trees and other things to see around the corner. I think it helped me because I'm more aware of what is around the corner.

***

Driver's Ed. enabled me to make better use of my mirrors and I am now able to check my blind spot more effectively. Braking is easier.

***

What sticks with me is the awareness. Constantly being aware of everything around you and anticipation of all that's happening is what I learned most. Of course I learned that directionals are mechanical and are subject to failure, but that should be a given to a driver with ½ a brain. Mr. M's has made me better at correcting situations while staying alert. And of course I use my brakes much less now.—Thanks.

***

What I learned:
- look over the shoulder before I get out
- to do hand over hand recovery
- to look at the mirror many times while driving
- to constantly check the road for danger points
- to look at the environment or road conditions at stoplights
- to honk horns when people can't see you

***

I now feel more easy to drive on highways.

***

I have learned how to notice an approaching situation, (i.e., I can see though the bushes that a car is backing out). I would honk the horn to warn him that I am passing by his driveway. In another instance, I noticed a bicyclist bicycling on the road on the right side. I would switch on my left directional and pull over to the left side of my lane to pass him, by driving more slowly.

***

Looking in the rear view mirror before coming to every stop. Signaling over a yellow line when passing a stopped vehicle in front of you. Checking blind spots when driving on a highway. How to come onto a highway properly without endangering anybody. How to avoid a ticket by driving a little slower than the rest of the traffic and where there are hills where you cannot see is a good place for a cop to be.

***

- Look in the rear view mirror when braking.
- Checking the entrance ramp or parkway to be aware of cars coming onto the highway.
- Let car settle down to avoid braking around turns.

***

Well, I basically learned that I can drive and that it is not hard as it seems. At the same time, it takes a lot of concentration and that driving is something that is serious and that when you drive, you should be responsible.

***

I learned many things in the driving portion of Driver's Ed.
1   I learned to always check the mirror before stopping.
2   Expect the unexpected:
   a) car doors to open.
   b) kids to run into the street, etc…
       1) cover brake when going through a school area or a parking lot.

3   Don't distract the driver.
4   Save gas by taking foot off of the accelerator when approaching a red light or stop sign.
5   Slow down when entering something with a minor curve. I learned this courtesy of another student.
6   Hand over hand recovery.
7   To notice the back of stop signs or other vehicles' stop signs. (I'm still working on this one.)

***

The driving portion of driver's ed was very informative to me. It taught me how to take care of my car, being a woman. I am now aware of how to make sure I will not be taken advantage of when getting my car repaired. It also taught me how to make sure I get my money's worth when I buy gas.

***

From The Author:

Thank you very much for taking the time to read this publication. The whole idea was a suggestion from one of my students.

He said, "Why don't you write a book, Mr. Myers?"

And so I did!

This Publication has been put together as food for thought only. Hear Say Items Have Not Been Removed. The Author's Opinions may differ from the opinion's of the readers, students and hear say. This Publication will improve the new driver's concept of safety. It is not to be taken or confused with a driver's manual.

"It is a Diary!"

As I put this last piece of information together, one student's comment comes to mind, "Driving is not a contact sport!"

This class was great and I am grateful to have taught them.

"You are the best generation yet."

I wish them all the luck in the world, and the stars if they choose to touch them!

0-595-28029-3